CAN EVERYONE PLEASE
PLEASE
CALM
DOWN?

First published in Great Britain in 2019 by Wren & Rook

ISBN: 978 1526361653
E-book ISBN: 978 1526361714

An Hachette UK Company
www.hachette.co.uk
www.hachettechildrens.co.uk

Publishing Director: Debbie Foy
Senior Editor: Laura Horsley
Art Director: Laura Hambleton
Designed by Thy Bui

Printed in England

CAN EVERYONE PLEASE CALM DOWN?

MAE MARTIN

CONTENTS

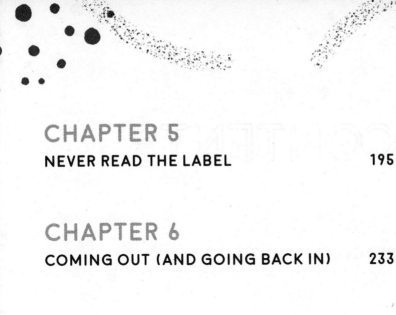

This book is dedicated to my parents, whose lack of squeamishness around sexuality imbued me with the confidence to be myself.

CHAPTER 1

21ST CENTURY SEXUALITY

HELLO

My first crush was Bette Midler, who is a woman. My
second crush was Clint Eastwood, who is a man. My
third was the character Frank N. Furter from *The Rocky
Horror Picture Show*, who is an alien transvestite.
Next it was Lumière from Disney's *Beauty and the
Beast*, who is a candlestick. My parents must have
known early on that my sexual tastes were going to
be varied. If there is a 'sexuality spectrum' – a range
of sexualities and attractions anyone can experience
– then I've probably existed at every point of that
spectrum at some point in my life. I've bounced
around it like a small yellow kernel of sweetcorn in
a sexual pinball machine (a decade ago someone
casually told me that my head resembles a kernel of
sweetcorn and I immediately internalised it for the
rest of my life).

So, welcome to my guide to 21st century sexuality. This is a book about human sexuality and its intended audience is, well, everyone! I've made my target audience 'every human being on the planet' firstly because it seemed inclusive, and secondly because it seemed financially savvy. Right off the top, I should explain that I am in NO WAY academically qualified to tackle a lofty thing like a 'Guide to 21st Century Sexuality'. In all honesty, I only recently learned that we are, in fact, living in the 21st century. There is an ever-increasing and exciting number of ways that people identify their sexualities, or gender identities, and I absolutely don't claim to be an expert on any of them. The whole arena of modern sexuality can seem like a minefield to even the most woke academic, and I'm well aware that I never even finished high school or went to university (that's not something I recommend, by the way – it puts a lot of pressure on your book to be a smash hit, because you don't have a 'real' job or steady income). Instead I became a comedian with a diploma in 'massage therapy' (a very strange choice for me) and an encyclopedic knowledge of Harry Potter trivia (you want to talk Horcruxes? Come at me, bro). But beyond Harry Potter trivia, if there is one area that I'm 100% at least anecdotally and personally qualified to explore, it's sexuality. (I tried to pitch a book on my only other area of expertise, 'how to make someone mad at you by repeatedly asking if they're mad at you', but publishers weren't interested. Actually, now that I think about it, I'm quite worried those publishers are mad at me ...)

I have short blonde hair – hence the earlier sweetcorn comparison, I dress androgynously and I talk pretty openly about dating people of all genders. Because of this, there's one question I get asked a LOT in interviews that are meant to be about my career, or my comedy: 'What are you?' In other words: 'At what part of the now exhaustive LGBTQI initialism do you exist?' and 'How do you identify, and why?' All anyone seems to want to know about anyone's sexuality is a one-word response – 'gay', 'bi' or another convenient soundbite – that can help them categorise things. These categories can be useful to help us communicate and foster a community, but isn't it more complicated than that? Not complicated in a pedantic or stressful way, but complicated in the beautiful, nuanced way that life is? Like the multi-layered plot of *The Lord of the Rings?*

At various points in my life I've been, I suppose, by definition: straight, gay, bi and pansexual. I've dated cisgender men and women, couples, trans people, asexual people. You name it, I've likely been there, looking for (and sometimes finding) love. Because mainly I'm attracted to funny people, and those exist across all categories. As a stand-up comedian, I've always been more interested in the human things that make us the same, not the labels that separate us. The kind of questions I want to ask are broader, like ...

Have you ever been in love?

Who was your first crush?

What turns you on?

How have your attractions changed over time?

What even is sexuality?

What's the weirdest sex dream you've ever had?

Have you had that one about Severus Snape and Buffy the Vampire Slayer having sex with you in a crypt?

Is that just me?

Really ...? Just me?

I've always had a tendency to over-share, I've made a career out of it, and I can tell you from experience that the weirdest, most specific, personal, embarrassing things I've talked about on stage always seem to be the things people relate to the most. That's the great prank life plays on us – the things we hide and are ashamed of would secretly be the most unifying things if only we said them out loud. They're the things that make us human.

It has always struck me as really strange that we ask people 'what' they are, instead of 'who' they are, so perhaps another potential motivation behind writing this book was to try to provide some handy answers for YOU to use if you ever get interrogated about how you identify or who you want to sleep with. All you need to do is memorise the entire book and calmly recite it to whoever asks the questions, ideally while maintaining eye contact without blinking. You'll probably only need the first few paragraphs until the questioner backs off. (You're welcome.)

WHAT IS SEXUALITY?

SEXUALITY. That word is going to come up a lot in this book. I wish there were more synonyms for it so I didn't have to repeat it so much but anyway: sexuality. We've all got one! And every single person's is unique, nuanced, personal and complicated. That's because one word covers such a broad spectrum and, in a nutshell, is about understanding the sexual feelings and attraction you feel towards those around you. Society has given us broad categories we can use to define and describe our various attractions, to help us communicate them. Some of the basic terms for sexuality you will likely recognise are:

HOMOSEXUAL:
someone attracted to
someone of their own sex/
gender – 'gay'

HETEROSEXUAL: someone
attracted to the opposite sex/
gender – 'straight'

BISEXUAL: historically this referred to
someone attracted to both men and women,
but these days this definition is sometimes
broadened to someone who has the potential
to be attracted to all genders (men, women,
nonbinary people, trans people, etc.)

QUEER: Queer is a cool one – it used to be used as a derogatory term for a gay person, but now it's been reclaimed by the LGBTQ+ community it has become an umbrella term that pretty much means 'not strictly straight'. I like it

PANSEXUAL: someone whose attractions are not limited or defined by biological sex, gender or gender identity

ASEXUAL: lacking in feelings of sexual attraction to others, not feeling desire for sexual activity

But there are many more – some which you'll find in the glossary at the end of this book and some that I might not even be aware of yet. This language can be really useful as a great starting point, but we also have to remember that every single person's sexuality is different and won't necessarily fit into a neat box. I've personally always been reluctant to label myself, probably because my unfathomably chill parents never asked me to! If, 'I'm not sure, Mom,' is good enough for Wendy, maybe it should be enough for everyone. (More on Wendy's chill later.)

So we know that everyone has a sexuality, right? And there are different ways of categorising it? Well my belief, based on my personal experience, and one that is shared by lots of clever people whose books I read before attempting to write this one, is that if we are open to it our sexualities can be completely dynamic. This means they can change over time according to influences, experiences, hormones and so on. It's not necessarily something that stays the same throughout our lives and that we can clearly bottle up. It's been said many times, but 'love is love is love, and so is sex' (I'm the only one that's ever said that), and the whole messy experience is confusing enough without having to worry about 'what' we are! Figuring out how we identify can be useful and fun, but feeling pressure from others to label it or allowing others to label us based on assumption seem to me like a waste of precious brain space – it can be anxiety-inducing for lots of people.

My hope with this book is that by sharing my own varied and occasionally humiliating adventures in sex, dating and identity, I'll be able to demystify sexuality and find some common ground with you, my valued reader. Along the way we'll try and tackle some of the bigger questions, like:

WHAT WOULD IT BE LIKE TO GO TO MAE MARTIN'S SCHOOL OF SEXUALITY?

ARE PEOPLE BORN GAY?

WHAT IS 'COMING OUT' AND SHOULD YOU HAVE TO DO IT?

AND, IN THE 21ST CENTURY, WHEN IT COMES TO SEXUALITY, CAN EVERYONE JUST PLEASE CALM DOWN ...?!

SEXUALITY

'UNDERSTANDING THE SEXUAL FEELINGS AND ATTRACTION YOU FEEL TOWARDS THOSE AROUND YOU.'

MY HEROES – WENDY AND JAMES

The heroes of this story are my parents, Wendy and James. They have always been, at least as far as I can tell, completely unbothered about sexuality, mine, theirs or anyone else's. If they had hushed, worried conversations about what to do about my varied attractions when I was growing up, I was never privy to them. That is, of course, how it should be. In my mind they were completely unruffled by my dating men and women, and never put pressure on me to label myself in any way. I think actually they were just much too busy worrying about the fact that I'd dropped out of school to become a comedian – they didn't have time to worry about whether I was gay, straight, bi or something else. On top of that, they're hippies. In fact, my parents are so open-minded when it comes to these topics that when I announced I was planning on writing this book, they were confused. 'It's 2018! What's the big deal? Surely by now everyone realises that sexuality is a fluid thing?' they mused. My mum even compiled a rough list of other topics that might be more worth exploring and sent it to me in an email.

» SUBJECT: Possible book ideas for Mae

Message:
- Famous Canadians (do people know Pamela Anderson is Canadian?)
- The Canadian wilderness (mosquitoes, etc. ...)
- Something about witches
- Space tourism
- Biography of Shiloh Jolie-Pitt

Love Mum

Homophobia and confusion around sexuality are so far removed from my parents' world that they thought mosquitoes might be a more pressing social issue.

Growing up it felt like that too. I was seriously lucky. It was never 'assumed' that I was straight and my parents were never fazed by the possibility that either myself or my brother would be something other than heterosexual. I've never really spoken to my parents about how their openness around these issues saved me a great deal of anxiety growing up. It's easy to forget to talk to your parents about the big stuff when you're busy talking to them about your tax returns or how you don't understand Brexit. So sitting down to write this book I found I had some questions about how they got to be so relaxed. Here is what my mum had to say …

'I was deeply engaged in the process of helping to form your spirit and your intellect – you'll remember how often we read together, went to museums etc. – but I felt that your sexuality was yours to form, like your identity, and that it was none of my business. I had gay friends at school and at university so it wasn't any big deal. I hate marginalisation of all kinds and labelling and judging and pigeon-holing. There is just so much more in this world to worry about than sex. I never made any assumptions at all about whether you would be gay or straight.'

Pretty great right? Well my dad is equally brilliant. Here's what he has to say about the sexual rainbow ...

THE SEXUAL RAINBOW

'There are far more blurred colours in the sexual rainbow than I ever really thought about before – more nuances of sexual taste and preference. Deny or repress these – in yourself or in someone else – and a life can become imbalanced, too preoccupied with this one (albeit profound and important) aspect of existence. If someone can find their sexual place in the world and be comfortable there then they can get on with the other important parts of life (being creative, useful, generous, kind, etc.) without always having to struggle to be understood – or to understand themselves.'

JAMES (MY DAD), 2018

TIMES ARE CHANGING: WHERE ARE WE NOW?

As you may have noticed, my parents are absolute dreamboats. But as I say, I know I was fortunate. I am well aware, through the experiences of many of my friends for a start, of the plenty of parents and families across the world that don't accept anything other than heterosexuality. It's still scary out there! The truth is, no matter how enlightened we might feel, LGBTQ+ rights are still under threat all over the world. Same-sex relationships are illegal in 72 countries, and there are 8 countries in which homosexuality can result in the death penalty. That's a pretty pressing human rights crisis, if you ask me. It's life or death.

It's worth remembering how easily we can slip backwards too, despite progress being made. Same-sex marriage was repealed in Bermuda, for instance, just after it was legalised! It remains an ongoing debate so I'm still crossing my fingers for a Bermuda beach wedding with Ariana Grande. I live in England, where, thrillingly, 'gay marriage' recently became legal. (I put it in quotation marks because now I think we're allowed to simply call it 'marriage'!) But at the same time, we are seeing worrying surges in hate crime. The unfortunate reality is that even in 2018, even in London, one of the most cosmopolitan cities in the world, if you 'look gay' (what does that even mean, please?), or your gender isn't immediately apparent, or you've ever walked down the street holding the hand of someone of the same sex, you will have experienced first-hand how far we still have to go socially before we reach a place of true equality. You might have had things shouted at you, felt people staring, felt a vague feeling of threat, or been asked inappropriately personal questions. These reactions

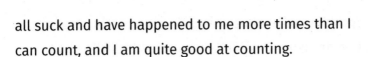

all suck and have happened to me more times than I can count, and I am quite good at counting.

It's tempting to think that equal marriage rights for all means equality for all. But, without wanting to sound negative, I would say legalising marriage for same-sex couples should be a benchmark of equality, not the end goal. The end goal of equality has got to be about eliminating the underlying squeamishness or distaste that some people still have around things like seeing same-sex affection. I've often heard people say things along the lines of 'Of course, I'm pro legal equality, but I don't need to see it in front of my face, two guys kissing. Ew.' THAT's what we need to sort out. We need to eradicate the sneaky homophobia that lurks in people's hearts (including our own!), and challenge the prejudices that can make us see anything other than heterosexuality as strange, different or weird. I'm here to prove that it could not be more natural and less weird.

No one can deny: times are changing, and the way we perceive and label sexuality is changing too. Here's some compelling evidence that we're heading in the right direction: more and more millennials (would that be a good band name? More and More Millennials?) are moving away from labelling their sexualities. I don't know how everyone else feels about that, but I find it super exciting! And a recent YouGov survey actually said that almost half of people in the UK between 18 and 24 no longer identify as either gay or straight.[1] They don't feel the need to label themselves. Just ask Miley Cyrus, Kristen Stewart, Josh Hutcherson or Tom Daley, all of whom have echoed this sentiment about sexual fluidity in interviews, and who incidentally are all former sexual partners of mine. (I'm JOKING, they're not, but I'm a highly ambitious and determined person so I'm not ruling it out at some perfect future date.)

By the time I've finished writing this PARAGRAPH there will probably be another letter added to the LGBTQIA (Lesbian, Gay, Bisexual, Transgender, Queer or Questioning, Intersex and Asexual) initialism. But right now, I think the initialism most people are going with is LGBTQ+ (the plus sign encompassing all the recent additions). It's a LOT to wrap your head around! Even I find it hard to keep up. I think part of the reason some people are so uncomfortable discussing sexuality is that whenever social issues evolve as quickly as this, we can experience a sense of vertigo – like we're travelling up a skyscraper in a glass lift – suddenly all dizzy and unsettled.

Something I've noticed is that when the subject of sexuality or gender comes up around my parents' or grandparents' generation, they kind of shut down. Their eyes glaze over and they start mumbling, 'LGBTQ – oh I just don't understand, it's all too much these days – Miley Cyrus says she DOESN'T HAVE a gender, I mean I ask you. What does she think she is, a bookcase?' I get that. I understand. I do. The amount of new information people of that generation are being asked to absorb is overwhelming. I remember having the exact-same feeling when my maths teacher introduced the idea of algebra in Grade 6. A creeping sense of frustration and panic, a lump rising in my throat, like, 'I've only JUST wrapped my head around NUMBERS and now you're introducing LETTERS? But why? X+Y? What is this unnatural witchcraft? I'm okay with these letters in theory but do they need to rub it in my face?' In fact, I almost immediately dropped out of school in rebellion. I bet if there had been an algebra pride march I would have gone and protested against it. If we feel an urge to throw our hands up, or storm out of a room when something is being explained to us, it's a pretty good indication of one thing – not that we reject the idea, but that we don't understand it, and that feeling of not understanding something scares us.

CHILL OUT

People are scared of change, even if the change appears to be common sense, like 'stop oppressing a certain group'. I mean, look at feminism. Until the recent cultural burst of enthusiasm for, and understanding of, feminism, SO many people were vocally reluctant or embarrassed to call themselves a feminist, simply because they found it all a bit overwhelming. They didn't understand that a 'feminist' doesn't mean somebody who hates men, it simply means someone who believes people of all genders deserve equal rights. The same goes for gay rights – people shut down because they don't understand that there's no scary gay agenda. Nobody is trying to erase straight people. The end goal is simple …

EQUAL HUMAN RIGHTS FOR ALL!

So, my main message is:

GUYS, CALM DOWN.

It's all going to be fine, and I truly believe that we're moving towards a place where sexuality is more inclusive and 'fluid' (that's a term I'm going to get stuck into later on). Sexuality is, in fact, much easier to understand than a super-long initialism. It's the most universal and human thing in the world.

My dream is that we get to a point where we don't even need to discuss sexuality! Yes I KNOW it's bizarre to be writing an entire book about the very thing I'm desperate for people not to feel the need to discuss. Honestly, though, I dream of a world where it's a total non-issue and everyone's falling in love with everyone all over the place with no stress involved. Seeing as we're far from there yet, however, I think it is incredibly important to explore it, out in the open, without embarrassment. I hope this book is a step in that direction. ENJOY. And please don't judge me too harshly. Before this, the longest thing I'd ever written was a tweet.

CHAPTER 2

MAE'S
SCHOOL OF
SEXUALITY

WHAT DO WE TEACH THE KIDS?

I'm pretty sure nobody is born with any kind of hang up about sexuality or gender. I've never met a baby with a particularly fully formed opinion on any social issue. When we're born, I believe, all we care about is poo and milk and crying. Our thoughts, feelings and opinions are largely formed in two main arenas: at home (by our families), and at school (by our teachers, who follow a curriculum, and our friends). It's these two places where our personalities and world views are built, and it's these two places I want to focus on in this chapter.

Little kids are like sponges. They soak up every offhand comment they hear and carefully store them with other crumbs in the pockets of their personalities (this is how sponges work, yes?). Everybody has their parents' voices running through their inner monologue in some way or another. Even if you can't immediately hear them, listen closely, their voices are there like a constant murmured chorus. Not just the lessons and instructions our parents directly give us as children ('don't run with scissors,' 'the bath and toilet are for different uses, please refrain from pooing in the bath'), but also their inadvertent slips. We soak up their subtle glances, the language they use, their physical/emotional/verbal cues and weird behaviours. These things get all tied up inside us, woven into the fabric of who we are. I'm sure, like everyone, I've inherited six million tiny and not-so-tiny neuroses and hang-ups from my parents, but in terms of instilling in me a totally judgement-free attitude to sex and sexuality my parents were **ABSOLUTE LEGENDS**. I mean sure, maybe one day I'll write a book called 'Why I wash my face five times a day and have a fear of abandonment', but this book is about sexuality and as I've mentioned, Wendy and James are the true heroes.

So if parents can imprint themselves on their children, whether we like it or not, they have a huge amount of power. I mean – they're shaping the leaders of tomorrow! Or, if that seems like too much pressure, the baristas and podcast hosts of tomorrow! It's an especially worrying thought for me because a lot of my friends have started having babies. It's seriously disconcerting seeing your friend's facial features reflected back at you in a fresh little human buddha. 'Will you, like your father, get drunk at a wedding, drop your phone in the outdoor composting toilet, and have to miss the speeches while you fish it out?' I wonder specifically as I look at my friend Sebastian's brand-new son …

I don't know yet if I want to have kids myself, but it would be fun to build their brains, wouldn't it? I can't think of a more fulfilling creative exercise. I think my mum felt that way, too. I remember her once getting me out of bed at about midnight, I was about ten years old, and asking if I wanted to go to the local cemetery, scale the fence, and get chased by the security guards just for fun. I did, obviously, and we did, and that was how I developed a sense of adventure, spontaneity and a healthy fear of German shepherd dogs. My mum's method of approaching parenting as a creative exercise also taught me so much more – like respect, resilience and humour – and as we'll see, she played a huge part in preventing me from stressing out about who I fall in love with.

WHY I'M NOT MATURE ENOUGH TO HAVE CHILDREN YET

1. I think the best first name for a baby is Susansarandon, all one word.

2. I had six spring rolls for breakfast and I'm about to order more spring rolls for lunch.

3. A month ago I lost my keys and I'm too scared to tell my flatmates because it's the fourth time it's happened, so I've been entering and exiting the house by secretly climbing through a back window via a drainpipe for four weeks.

4. A few pages ago I referred to the process of parenting as 'building their brains".

5. I instigate spin the bottle at EVERY party, regardless of whether it's a house party or a sit-down meal with a cheese plate and people's older relatives present.

AN
EXPLOSION
OF RAINBOWS

So we're all agreed I'm not ready for kids just yet, but hey I can still have an opinion about how everyone **ELSE** raises their kids, right? The first time I remember hearing about sex was a conversation I had with my mum at five years old. **FIVE YEARS OLD**. How big is a five-year-old? Small, right? Like three inches tall? Roughly the size of a toy you get in a Kinder egg? Well it must have been an incredibly impactful conversation because I remember it so vividly. I remember sitting down on our old grey sofa, dusty shafts of light streaming through the window, and feeling a distinct sense that stuff was about to get real. The table was adorned with hand-drawn diagrams (hand-drawn! Why? Get a book from the library, surely?) and she said, 'This is how a man and a woman have sex, and this is how a man and a man have sex, and a woman and a woman ...' – she covered **ALL** the bases! Incredible. After covering the different ways any combination of people could have sex, she also informed me, calmly, that there was no Santa Claus (sorry if this is news to you). All of this, in **ONE** conversation! All my friends' parents despised me because on the first day of school I ruined Christmas for the whole class ... and told them about anal sex.

But I am so grateful that in that first conversation about the birds and the bees, the gay birds and the lesbian bees were given equal footing. (Nobody ever mentioned the bisexual beetles or the asexual crickets, but hey, they did their best.) It meant that I always felt that same-sex relationships were normal, and that my parents weren't disturbed by them in the slightest.

Did my parents sometimes go too far in their open-mindedness? Maybe. Once you commit to being totally open about sex and sexuality you're sure to run into some problems – for instance, in that same, all-encompassing conversation, age five, my mum told me what an orgasm is. Giving me all the info was a positive impulse for sure, but the way my mum explained it was bizarre and I held on to it for many years. To help me wrap my head around it, her explanation of orgasms was steeped in imagery and symbolism. She said, 'When two people love each other and they're naked, and having sex, they feel very happy, and then they feel increasingly happy, and finally they reach a moment of extreme happiness' and (I still can't believe this is what she went with) 'an explosion of rainbows cascades across the sky'. An **EXPLOSION OF RAINBOWS**. Readers who have not yet experienced an orgasm, I must warn you: there are a lot fewer prisms than you might expect. Imagine my disappointment … when the time finally came … and there were no rainbows in sight. Just the general sense of existential intensity that occasionally follows, and a real hunger for chips.

One of the first full-length films I was ever shown was the genderbending rock musical *The Rocky*

Horror Picture Show. Again, I was five years old. (Apparently my parents had decided this was the right age to be exposed to not some, but all of the facts of life.) My tiny mind, hidden under a choppy bowl-cut, was **BLOWN**. The film is a family favourite – my dad grew up in London and used to watch it live on stage at the Royal Court Theatre in the 1970s, when it was the hottest ticket in town, with Mick Jagger and David Bowie vying for seats. In fact, my grandfather was an actor and played 'the narrator' in the stage production! I think at the time it came out it was considered controversial, for sure, but not as controversial as you might imagine considering it debuted more than 45 years ago and is essentially a story about a bisexual alien transvestite mad scientist who creates a living muscle man in his laboratory to be his sex slave. Yep, if you haven't watched it yet, you're in for a treat. Things were pretty groovy back then. It's crazy to think that in the 1990s, when I was a pre-teen, people freaked out about a single chaste gay kiss in the hottest teen soap opera of the time – *Dawson's Creek*! In the Bowie-steeped 70s, androgyny and masculinity co-existed happily, and London was teeming with men in platform shoes and eyeliner, my dad included. In fact, I believe my father was the lead singer of a rather flamboyant glam rock band in the 70s called 'Johnny Eagle and the Evil Smelling Stink Show', but that's another story.

I remember watching the film wide-eyed as Tim Curry tossed his cape aside to reveal his fishnet stockings, corset and slim muscular body. He was a vision of virility, raw sexuality and power. 'Is he a man or a woman?' I asked. 'Sort of ... both?' my dad replied. I remember a short debate about whether we should fast-forward through the scene where Frank N. Furter, silhouetted behind a curtain, has sex with both Janet and then Brad in quick succession. It was decided that I could handle it. My eyes grew wider as I watched. 'Is he gay or straight?' I asked. 'Sort of ... neither,' my dad replied again. From that moment on I knew that there was a world of possibility out there, and that Tim Curry was a god. He was living the ultimate dream, unanimously desired and idolised by both men and women. My teachers, however, were less open-minded when I tried to teach my Grade 1 class the lyrics to 'Sweet Transvestite' on the playground the next day ...

'THE BEST TIME OF YOUR LIFE'

You may have heard people say 'enjoy school, these are the best days of your life'. I certainly heard that a lot. And if you're still in education, you may be thinking you're doing it wrong if you find that actually, school is nothing like the earth-shatteringly romantic experience American teenagers seem to be having in films. You might look around your classroom and think, 'I would never in my life actively choose to socialise with any of these absolutely appalling people.' That's okay too. It's not for everyone. Going to school was a shock to my system in a lot of ways, especially because I had no idea that the rest of the world wasn't as open-minded as my family.

When I arrived at school in Grade 1, I instantly bonded with a girl called Karen. We were both premature and I guess we were also both quite weird. I was five years old, having skipped kindergarten and missed out on acquiring crucial kindergarten skills in the process (I still don't know how to colour-in or share with others), and the rest of the girls were six. It was an all-girls' school and in those first few weeks it seemed to me like most of the girls were a different species to me. I'd been raised to hate Barbies, and my hair was cut, at my request, to look exactly like my older brother's (the shape of a bowl). My uniform didn't seem to fit right and I was constantly tugging at my tights. I rarely wore dresses at home, so it felt weird wearing one every day. The other girls were well put together, with plastic butterfly clips holding their long, shiny hair neatly in place. They were at ease with themselves like the girls in children's books. They had all the right stationery. Glitter-pens. Giltter-tape. Glitter-glue. Protractors and compasses in shiny boxes. Those giant erasers that say 'For BIG Mistakes'. I used a plastic bag as a rucksack and my locker was filled with weeks of old packed lunches, cheese sandwiches and apples, like I was preparing for some kind of apocalypse.

Karen was messy and disorganised like me. Plus we both liked Bette Midler and had imaginary friends who were dogs which all seemed like good things to bond over at the time. We hung out every break for the first two weeks and played imaginary games like 'Pippi Longstocking' (she played the protagonist, Pippi, a pig-tailed adventurer who traversed the globe in a hot-air balloon, and I alternated between playing her submissive male sidekick Tommy, and her pet monkey Mr Nillson). Anyway, one day we were under a table playing one of these imaginary games, and everything was lovely, and I guess I was overwhelmed by the loveliness of it all and I kissed her hand. The plot of the game warranted it! I was in character! I don't remember the details, but I do remember that somebody saw us and instantly a mob of six-year-old girls formed around us. '**EEEEWWW.** Mae kissed Karen!!!' They ran to get the teacher. Instead of running away, I remember following behind them, bemused. Why would they tell the teacher? What had I done wrong? My teacher, the angelic Mrs Khatri (a wild-haired chain-smoking woman with many scarves ... sort of an Indian Helena Bonham Carter), was unfazed and told the rest of the class, in so many words, to stop being dickheads and leave us the hell alone. It was eye opening, though, and I remember being stressed and upset. Karen and I drifted apart after that. Things like that happen all the time, leaving us kids feeling confused, ashamed and embarrassed. How had a group of six-year-olds already absorbed the (false) idea that two girls kissing is weird? And how early, in classrooms all over the world, are the creeping tendrils of shame, the feelings of 'otherness' and self-loathing, taking root in kids' faultless little souls?

I am lucky because that incident with Karen was an anomaly for me. It's a strange little cactus in my memory. Later on, the reaction I got at home from my parents when they figured out I wasn't strictly straight was devoid of panic, fear and pessimism, so I luckily felt relatively convinced that this update to my sexuality felt like a non-issue. When I **DID** eventually have to face the fact that the world does not necessarily feel the same way as Wendy and James, I was confident in my belief that there was nothing wrong with me. A sense of righteousness and a lack of self-loathing had already been embedded, and it worked, and still works, most of the time, as a kind of shield. I say most of the time because, of course, like most people who are visibly/openly not straight, the repetitive and constant onslaught of pebbles of homophobia has cracked that shield over time in subtle ways. It's impossible not to feel a sense of otherness in a world that has only recently recognised your equal legal rights, your humanity.

But how superhuman would I feel if I had encountered the same open-mindedness I encountered at home, at my school? Or if I had even been taught something in school about LGBTQ+ history, or same-sex relationships? Stories that I'm sure even my parents were/are unaware of? Well I'm going to attempt to write my own rough, poorly researched, and occasionally quite sexy curriculum that I think we **SHOULD** be taught in schools that would make the whole experience so much more fulfilling and empowering. **HERE WE GO.**

MAE'S FIT CURRICULUM

A friend of mine who's currently pregnant said to me
the other day, 'I'm so glad that my baby is going to be
born into the most socially and sexually progressive
world thus far in human history.' (She didn't say
'thus', I'm paraphrasing, I would never be friends with
anyone who said 'thus'. I once removed a friend from
my life because they used the word 'verily'.) I didn't
want to correct my friend, because I'm not a jerk and I
want her to be hopeful about the world she's bringing
human life into, but this is not the first or even the
most sexually progressive period in history. Although
things are definitely better now than they have been
in many years, and we can all freely watch Ru Paul
and the *Queer Eye* guys without fear of judgement,

sexual freedom is actually not a modern phenomenon at all! There are so many periods in ancient and not-so-ancient history when people have taken a much more open-minded view of sexuality and gender than we do even today.

Can I just take this moment to clarify something once again? I am not a historian or an expert, I am just a Wikipedia wizard. But this is my understanding of a smattering of gay history:

I mean, sure. Yes. For the past 2,000 years or so it's been pretty crappy to be gay. Like just constantly getting thrown in jail or killed level of crappy. Real poo town. So a good percentage of the stories we hear about gay people in recent history are tragic stories. Persecution, homophobia, imprisonment and so on. Let's take Alan Turing, for instance. A brilliant mathematician whose job it was to decipher military codes used by Germany and its allies during the Second World War. His crucial work cracking the Enigma Code probably shortened the war by two years and saved over 14 million lives. But despite that remarkable achievement, when I hear the name Alan

Turing another part of his legacy springs to mind and that's because the government he helped to save went onto charge him with being gay. They chemically castrated him and he ultimately committed suicide days before his 42nd birthday in the most tragically poetic way possible – by eating an apple laced with cyanide. Bleak. These kinds of awful stories are the ones we hear as children and they embed themselves in our brains so that we associate an LGBTQ+ lifestyle with hardship, gut-wrenching tragedy and darkness. It's having these stories drilled into us that makes parents respond to their kids coming out by saying, 'Oh, I'm just worried that life will be much harder for you.' What kind of message does that send to someone? 'I'm just worried about how hard it'll be for you' is basically saying 'I'd rather you were straight because you'd probably be happier.' Not exactly a positive outlook. 'Oh cool thanks, Mum and Dad. I guess I'll start looking forward to my apparently miserable life. Can't wait.'

How different would things be if we started focusing on the positive? If we were made aware from an early age that …

AS LONG AS THERE'S BEEN SEX. THERE'S BEEN ALL KINDS OF SEX.

It's a huge part of our experience as humans on this planet and history is crammed full of highly successful people who were LGBTQ+. There has been a tradition of omission – or, as I call it, a 'tradish of omish' – when it comes to sexuality. Known secrets and tactful silence. Referring to people's lifelong partners as their 'friends' or 'roommates' just to avoid embarrassment (or, I suppose until recently, imprisonment). At times when I was growing up, when I was submerged in the curriculum of my religious all-girls' school and *The Rocky Horror Picture Show* had faded to an indistinct shadow in my memory, I'm sure I thought there were only two gay people in history: Oscar Wilde and Ellen DeGeneres. I tried to model myself on both of them at various points, an effort that led to a lot of bad blazers and worse poetry. My history teachers and textbooks deleted the sexualities of all the other supremely influential, great and accomplished people who have had documented same-sex relationships. Are you ready to unearth a few?

THE MOST EPIC LIST OF ALL TIME

I hereby present you with an absolutely epic list of notable and brilliant people from the vaults of history who are thought to have had same-sex relationships:

- LEONARDO DA VINCI
- TENNESSEE WILLIAMS
- MARLON BRANDO
- TCHAIKOVSKY
- VIRGINIA WOOLF
- LORD BYRON
- BILLIE HOLIDAY
- SIR FRANCIS BACON
- WALT WHITMAN
- JANIS JOPLIN

- MICHELANGELO
- ISAAC NEWTON
- ALEXANDER THE GREAT
- KING JAMES I
- ELEANOR ROOSEVELT
- JAMES DEAN
- EMILY DICKINSON
- FRIDA KAHLO
- JULIUS CAESAR
- WHITNEY HOUSTON

It's a kind of a who's who of influential or iconic people when you think about it and it shows us that though it can sometimes seem that gay people in history lived on the fringes of culture and society, in reality, they played a huge part in shaping the world as we know it! In fact, I now want to go back through all my textbooks with a pen and add in all the great untold same-sex love stories. But I can't. So I'm writing this book instead.

ENGLISH LITERATURE WITH BRANDO

I always remember an English literature teacher of mine showing us *A Streetcar Named Desire* when I was about 13. For anyone who hasn't watched it, it's a steamy drama from 1951 starring a young Marlon Brando (in his absolute prime) as the passionate and volatile Stanley Kowalski. Brando – influential actor, icon, total dreamboat and activist for numerous causes – prowls around the screen like a panther in a sweaty tank top, all muscle and brooding angst. Our teacher was profoundly obsessed with him (and Pierce Brosnan ... she had a framed photo of Pierce Brosnan on her desk that she used to sigh wistfully at while we worked but that's a different story). Before we watched *A Streetcar Named Desire* I remember her sitting on the edge of her desk with her legs crossed, swinging her feet coquettishly, her eyes glazing over as she delivered a short but passionate monologue about how Brando expressed himself through his raw masculinity and sexual energy. To her, he was the ultimate alpha heterosexual male – dominant, powerful and stereotypically 'manly'.

Years later I found out that the label of the ultimate heterosexual male wouldn't have fitted Brando at all. Brando was actually a sexual omnivore, openly bi, who had relationships with men as well as women. I couldn't believe it. I feel like if my teacher had known that her ultimate sex god, Marlon Brando, had gay tendencies she would have been a bit more vigilant about reprimanding all the kids in the class who used 'that's so gay' as an insult, an expression that many teachers at the time seemed to turn a blind eye to. (Unfortunately

'THAT'S SO GAY'

is still a phrase thrown around with little thought, particularly in schools, in which 'gay' is used to connote something weak, uncool or bad. It's lazy, it's insulting, and I hope teachers everywhere call it out wherever they encounter it. I had a friend in my mid-20s who would fairly regularly slip up and say 'that's so gay' about anything from a late train to an ugly shirt. She assured me it was just an expression and that I shouldn't be offended, so I asked her every time she was tempted to say 'that's so gay' about something crappy, to imagine saying 'that's so Mae' instead. That helped her understand how dispiriting it felt to me.

Marlon Brando slept with almost every young starlet of his time, but on top of that, the list of his male partners is so hot I can't even deal with it. Think the great and the good of cinema in the 50s and 60s: Burt Lancaster, Laurence Olivier, John Gielgud, Noël Coward, Tyrone Power, Rock Hudson and Montgomery Clift (on a dare, he and Clift once ran naked down Wall Street together). And only recently did the widow of the comedian Richard Pryor confirm that he and Brando were lovers too! Last but not least, the actor and cultural icon James Dean (another obsession of my horny English teacher) and Brando are reported to have had a tumultuous affair as well. I can't imagine a better pairing for an erotic fan fiction than Brando and Dean – the Rebel Without a Cause himself. 'Brando appeared in the doorway of Dean's trailer, his broad shoulders blocking out the light. His eyes moved over Dean's slight frame.' Actually, I need to take a break from my laptop and have a glass of water.

I'm back. When Brando was at the top of his game, many men in Hollywood, including some of his lovers, were in the closet. I wish I could say that isn't the case anymore, but I think it probably still is. But Brando was unusual in that he was relatively open about his sexuality. He said in an interview, 'Like a large number of men, I, too, have had homosexual experiences, and I am not ashamed. I have never paid much attention to what people think about me.' **HOT!** Yet as I said, Brando was the exception rather than the rule and it's still hard to imagine an A-Lister discussing this in such an open way now without it becoming a massive media storm. I'll talk more about this and about the importance of visibility in the chapter about 'coming out', but I do really believe that if we learned from a young age how many LGBTQ+ people had shaped the world we live in, if we had a greater number of strong role models, then we'd perhaps start to hear 'that's so gay' in a different context. Maybe people would use that phrase to describe a winning Olympic performance, or a well-tailored suit, or a new scientific discovery. 'Hey, did you hear that quantum physicists have finally figured out how an atom can exist in two places at once?' 'Oh my God! That's so gay!'

A LONG, LONG

TIME AGO ...

THE EMPEROR'S NEW SLEEVE

Gay history isn't limited to the liberal Hollywood elite. In ancient China, homosexuality was openly acknowledged and relatively normal, especially among men. We are talking THOUSANDS of years ago, here. It wasn't labelled as 'homosexuality' back then of course, that's a recent term. In fact there were all kinds of euphemisms and expressions used instead, my favourite of which is 'the passion of the cut sleeve'. I'm going to start using that as a pick-up line. 'Hey, are you interested in engaging in the passion of the cut sleeve?' (I'll be single and celibate my whole life.)

Actually the origin of that phrase is **EXTREMELY** romantic. Let me tell you that story:

This is one of my favourite same-sex love stories, which I read about in a **GREAT** book called *A Little Gay History*. It's the story of Emperor Ai (27–1 BCE) in the Han Dynasty and his love for Dong Xian, a married man and member of his court. It's written about Emperor Ai that he 'did not care for women'. This was a well-known fact. The Emperor loved the lads. This wasn't particularly unusual at the time. In fact, a famous Chinese scholar named Pan Guangdan came to the conclusion that nearly every emperor in the ancient Chinese Han Dynasty had one or more male sexual partners. Anyway the story goes that one night he was sleeping next to Dong Xian, with Dong Xian stretched out across one of the Emperor's long sleeves. The Emperor was awake and being called to a meeting, but he didn't want to wake up his sleeping bf so, rather than disturbing him, he actually cut off his own sleeve, so that Dong Xian could continue sleeping on it. How romantic is that? **SO ROMANTIC**. The most romantic thing anyone has ever done for me is spontaneously offer me their last French fry, and that was a taxi driver who really should have been watching the road. Regardless, I'm tearing up at the memory.

The fact that this story about the Emperor and the sleeve is written about affectionately by a member of the court speaks volumes about the level of acceptance even 2,000 years ago. Not total acceptance, though. Emperor Ai actually tried to legally appoint Dong Xian as his successor, but was prevented by the court. For all the good in the world, we humans often fall short – then and now – when it comes to acknowledging same-sex love in the eyes of the law. (More on this later.)

ALEXANDER THE GREAT

When I was growing up, lesbian characters in movies
and on the television were aggressive predatory
gym teachers in khaki trousers and baseball hats,
or sad clowns yearning after straight women, and
bisexual women were depicted as nymphomaniac
psychos. Male gay characters were mostly flamboyant
wedding planners, hairdressers, florists or victims of
lynchings. Not that there's anything wrong with being
a hairdresser or a florist! But varied representation is
important because it reminds us that we can occupy
more than one small corner of the world. It would
have been such welcome news to me to discover that
one of the greatest military leaders in history was
arguably not straight.

Which brings us to Alexander the Great (356–323 BCE). He was one of the greatest military leaders in history, and changed the shape of the ancient world. He led his army to victories across the Persian Empire and by the age of 25 had become king of Macedonia, leader of the Greeks, overlord of Asia Minor and pharaoh of Egypt. He then went onto found more than 70 cities and create the largest empire the ancient world had ever witnessed – all in little over a decade! How inadequate are you feeling right now? All I've done today is learn the first three notes of *The Simpsons* theme song on the piano. I then filmed it and sent it to four friends, became tired, and had a nap. Just think how much Alexander got done in a day, and how valuable would it be for a young boy who thinks he might be attracted to men to read that it is thought that Alexander the Great was, in fact, probably not straight? Alexander the Great! Not straight!

Yep, that's right. Though Alexander had several well-documented relationships with women, some historians believe his relationship with his boyhood friend Hephaestion was probably also sexual. Their tutor, Aristotle, described their intense closeness as 'one soul abiding in two bodies'. But in 324 BCE, Hephaestion became ill with a fever. Alexander remained by his side until he showed signs of recovery, but once he left Hephaestion relapsed and passed away. Alexander was so grief-stricken he ordered a period of mourning throughout the empire and employed a famous artist to design the funeral pyre for Hephaestion. The pyre was very tall and built in stepped levels. Alexander gave orders that the sacred flame in the temple should be extinguished – something that was only done on the death of a great king, and a waaay more elaborate gesture than anything Alexander did in honour of his wives or girlfriends. When I die I would like to have a 200-feet-high funeral pyre built, please. And potentially a reenactment of the Battle for Hogwarts. (I have a feeling my future partner will probably just put my ashes out with the recycling.)

How amazing is it that the leader of one of the greatest, most powerful armies in human history is likely to have lived as openly bisexual? And how depressing is it that it took until 2011, only a few years ago, for America to allow openly gay people to serve in the military?! Even more upsetting – just a few months after Donald Trump became president of the United States (I still find it deeply disturbing to utter that phrase) he tried to ban transgender individuals from the military – something he is still trying to pursue. Where did everything go so wrong?

ANCIENT ROME

And what about ancient Rome? They were having the gayest time! Most high-school educations include a pretty detailed study of ancient Rome, where much of Western culture developed. But I don't remember ever learning about the sexual practices of the time and they're very interesting. In fact it's almost harder to find a Roman emperor who WAS heterosexual than one who was not. For example, at least two Roman emperors were in open same-sex relationships. Thirteen of the first 14 Roman emperors were thought to be bisexual or homosexual. Emperor Hadrian was famously devoted to his boyfriend Antinous for whom he built monuments after his death and for whom he mourned intensely. And did you know that

Emperor Nero married his boyfriend? He had a state wedding, a proper official wedding, and all the citizens were totally on board, they lined the streets in celebration. It was essentially a massive gay wedding with all the solemnity and ritual of matrimony and nobody was protesting, nobody had signs like 'It's Adam and Eve not Adam and Steve!' In fact, people would probably have been like 'Who the hell are Adam and Eve? We're just trying to celebrate our Emperor's marriage, thank you very much.'. I mean, to be fair, Nero was a murderous psychopath so it would have been a bad idea to interrupt his wedding with any kind of protest. But still.

We can't say for sure what the prevailing attitudes towards sexuality were at the time because, back then, the Romans didn't think of it in terms of 'sexuality'. They were very into dividing the acts from the person engaging in them.

That is,

SOMEONE WHO HAD SEX WITH BOTH MEN AND WOMEN WOULDN'T 'IDENTIFY' AS BISEXUAL ... IT WAS JUST SOMETHING THEY DID.

It's pretty unbelievable that, at least for men back then, people were less concerned with heteronormative sex than perhaps we are now.

It's fair to say we had some seriously progressive ancients but it begs the question, how did we end up with all this homophobia centuries later, and where does homophobia come from in the first place? I asked Dr Meg-John Barker, an author, academic, activist, psychotherapist and hero of mine. I'll be asking Dr Barker to chime in throughout this book because they are generally a million times more articulate than I am ...

'I'd say it comes from the heteronormative worldview that says that we're all binary: men or women who are either attracted to the 'opposite sex' (straight) or the 'same sex' (gay) (with men being seen as more 'normal' than women, and straight people more 'normal' than gay people). The history of that lies in the scientific project of trying to categorise everyone in relation to gender, sexuality, race, class, disability and many other things, often to justify treating some groups of people much worse than others.'

It also seems to me that when people are violently and outspokenly homophobic, it often reflects an unconscious conflict within themselves. By directing their aggression at LGBTQ+ people it somehow eases the anxiety they feel in themselves about similar or analogous feelings. Several recent scientific studies have reflected this idea, and a study in 1996 found that openly homophobic straight men showed an 'increase in penile erection' when showed gay male erotica that was significantly more distinct than non-homophobic straight men.[2] I'm not saying that every homophobe is gay, that would be too neat, and we know that homophobic feelings can arise from any number of sources – our parents, our culture, religion, etc. But anecdotally and instinctively we can see that, in many cases, self-hatred can lead people to join the very movements that would do them harm if they were open about themselves. A quick google of 'openly anti-gay/homophobic leaders who turned out to be gay or bi' will yield a list more than 20 names long, and still growing all the time. Maybe it's an extension of that old 'playground mentality' that's often used as an excuse for mistreatment, the fact that people bully the very people they desperately want to snog under the bleachers.

Although we might feel we live in inclusive times, the crazy thing is, prior to us labelling and policing sexuality and gender, it seems that all over the world, throughout all recorded ancient history, on nearly every continent, many thriving cultures have recognised and often revered diversity in gender and sexuality. The tricky part when looking at same-sex relationships throughout ancient history is a lack of primary sources (direct first-hand accounts or official documents): in general, the only documents we have outlining intimate relationships from the past are marriage records. Marriage in the ancient world was very much an economic contract, a business deal. We don't keep 'official records' of every time someone falls in love, or has hot sex next to a pyramid or in a Roman bath. If I died tomorrow I'd be officially remembered as a single woman, never married. History would remember me as 'Mae Martin – virgin spinster'. Nobody would remember that I once made out with someone while treading water in a lake in

Northern Ontario in the middle of the night, or any of the times that I've fallen in love – which incidentally feels a lot like making out in a lake in Northern Ontario. (I'm not, by the way, advocating that everyone runs out and starts having sexual encounters in bodies of water in Canada by moonlight. It's not for everyone, especially if you're not a strong swimmer. But it was great for me. I was about 20 at the time and my girlfriend and I were feeling incredibly moved by an unexpected sighting of a blue heron by the shore – the moment took us.) Luckily, though, we do have enough historical evidence through art, and written histories, to know for certain that same-sex love and desire have always been part of the human experience. Little to none of the history of variances in human sexuality is taught in schools but maybe we'd change one or two minds if it were.

MAE'S SEXUAL GEOGRAPHY

It's not just the ancients that accepted and even celebrated sexual diversity either. Let's take a look at some other cultures too:

SAMOA:

One of the arguments against homosexuality (particularly by far-right religious extremists – they **LOVE** this one) is that it is 'destructive to the family'. So it's interesting to note that homosexuality being 'outside' the family is a Western idea. There's a group in Samoan culture called the Fa'afafine who identify as a third gender. They are usually biologically male, but exhibit feminine traits and have sexual relationships with men. Not only are they completely socially accepted in Samoan culture, there's an expectation among Samoans that the fa'afafine are the glue that brings the family together. They take care of the children, and help to raise their nieces and nephews.

FIRST NATIONS:

In North America there's a two-spirit Zuni tradition, where a person lives as, and possesses the characteristics of, both masculinity and femininity simultaneously. Two-spirit people play a key role in society as mediators, priests and artists.

THE INCAS:

The South American Inca people worshipped chuqui chinchay, a dual-gendered god. They also recognised a third gender, who were often revered shamans (mystic healers) and wore androgynous clothing. Then the Spanish conquerors arrived, deemed them 'sodomites' and killed them. Cool, cheers, guys.

SIBERIA:

In Siberia, the Chukchi people are a nomadic, shamanic people who embrace a third gender. The third gender are assumed to be male at birth but sometimes marry men, and adopt female roles as well as male ones. They accompany men on the hunt, and take care of the family.

HAWAII:

In Hawaii, a multiple-gender tradition exists among the indigenous society. The 'Mahu' can be regarded as male or female at birth, but grow up to inhabit a gender role somewhere between or encompassing both the masculine and feminine. Their social role is sacred as educators of ancient traditions and rituals.

This is just the briefest of overviews, on top of this there were also ancient Sumerian cultures who recognised multiple genders, 'female husbands' in Western Kenya, matriarchal societies, cultures with bisexual deities and hermaphroditic gods. I think it's important to remember and recognise the rich history of diversity in gender and sexuality in different cultures. It helps us to understand what is generally accepted by academics: that sexuality, and the way people express it, is strongly affected by cultural norms. For example, the influence of centuries of patriarchal society (society led and driven by men) means that many modern societies are 'heteronormative', where gender roles are often strict, and male dominance and possession of female sexuality have historically been the norm. But it's so important to remember that it hasn't necessarily always been this way, that in other parts of the world throughout history, things have been different and may well be again in the future. Luckily, 'cultural norms' (or what we consider to be 'normal') shift and change all the time according to economics, new developments and opinions, and politics. What is 'normal' is not an unchanging equation, but fluid as a fashion trend. I mean, in the past cocaine was used as a cure for toothache, crocodile poo was used as a contraceptive (google it), and people used to iron their hair. Things change. So I'm just holding tight, waving my banner when I can, and crossing my fingers that we're moving in a direction where things are a little less binary and a little more groovy.

SEXY SCIENCE

I've often looked back and thought that, actually, I
don't remember learning ANYTHING except very basic
anatomy in school sex-ed. Certainly nothing about the
spectrum of unique sexual identities and attractions.
I do remember spending roughly three weeks learning
about how to build an effective parachute for an egg. I
definitely learned about the circumference of a circle,
and how to 'solve for x' in an equation. That all kept
us pretty busy I suppose. And on top of this, we spent
almost two weeks of my sociology class watching the
BBC series of *Pride and Prejudice* on a tiny TV screen
at the front of the class, solely because my teacher
fancied Colin Firth. Come to think of it, Mr Darcy
emerging from a lake with nothing but a wet white
shirt and skintight leggings on was probably the

closest we got to any kind of substantial sex ed.
Not ideal.

I had a health teacher in school called Ms Adams
whose job I suppose should have been to teach us
about sex. She spent an entire term talking about
the dangers of smoking – we did projects on it, she
smoked a cigarette in class to demonstrate (weird?)
but in two years she never once mentioned sexuality.
Which is doubly ironic because it was a known
secret among the students, parents and staff at the
school that she had been in a long-term clandestine
relationship with our history teacher Ms. Winters. I'm
not suggesting that, like the smoking, she should have
brought Ms Winters in to demonstrate, but it would
have been nice to at least broach the topic. Surely it's
time our curricula were expanded to include sex and
relationships of all kinds? Surely we should be told
something? Something positive? So that we don't go
on to live in decades-long secret relationships with
our colleagues ...?

Despite the fact that my parents made sexuality
a total non-issue in our house, there is still tons

of stuff that I wish I had been taught. Why is it so threatening to people, the idea of teaching kids about different sexualities? What are we worried will happen? A massive gay-athon in the streets? I think the perception that same-sex attraction is unnatural largely comes from the idea that sex is PURELY intended for reproduction. 'This phallic thing fits into this hole, and that's because sex is to make babies.'

I think (I hope!) we all know by now that that's not exactly the case. Sex **DOES** often result in babies of course, but it also serves so many more functions in society than just baby making. Having sex releases endorphins (happy brain chemicals) and strengthens social bonds. Love is also proven to make us live longer, happier, fuller, more productive lives. A society full of love is a strong society, and procreation is just one part of why we all want to bone each other left, right and centre. I can promise you that when I fooled around with Rodovan Popovic in high school I wasn't thinking about having his Dorito-eating, hair gelled babies. I was simply forming a social bond and enjoying an age-old pastime ... It was a significant night for me as it was the night I first saw the movie *The Matrix*, and the eve of 'Y2K', when everyone thought the world might end as we entered the year 2000. So, a potential apocalypse was making everything feel quite profound, and I felt very **VERY** close to Rodovan.

GAY ANIMALS

And how does the theory that being gay is unnatural account for all the gay animals in the world? They did a study recently of 1,500 different animal species and they found instances of bisexuality in ALL of them.[3] Animals are super gay sometimes, guys. In fact, no species has been found without homosexual behaviour, with the exception of species that never have sex at all, such as sea urchins and aphids. Elephants – you should see the things they do with their trunks. Remarkable. Penguins, swans, dolphins … The bonobo ape, our closest genetic relative, is almost exclusively bisexual. Female monkeys will often have sex with each other to resolve disputes, or just to pass the time.

I did a stand-up show recently and talked about gay animals, and somebody who'd been in the audience sent me a news article afterwards bearing this headline: 'Lesbian goat' (already amazing) 'partners with female goose and raises her chicks with her ...' Just a committed lesbian goat/goose couple. What could be better?

My favourite news headline this month was:

'Blind bisexual goose dies at age 40 after being stuck for years in a love triangle with a couple of swans.'

I laughed for 45 minutes when I read that. It just couldn't be any more suited to my sense of humour. I have so many questions. First of all, how do we know the goose was 40 years old? Who was monitoring his age? How do we know he was 'stuck' in the love triangle and not a willing participant? Poor guy.

If we want to create a world where we are all understood and respected as equals, we have to take an active interest in LGBTQ+ history and make sure we learn about how natural same-sex attraction is. We have to start chatting to each other about this stuff, from a very young age, before little creeping tendrils of shame start to infect our thoughts on same-sex love.

Let's be honest, sex education in schools isn't something we can rely on so we've got to create the conversations ourselves. And if and when we start having kids of our own, it's so important we talk to them openly too. Even if you tell them an orgasm is an explosion of rainbows cascading across the sky, we need to have the awkward conversations and demystify sex. That way, no one will waste years feeling anxious about who they should kiss or fall in love with. If we can make sexuality something no one has to worry about, we just free up more mental space to be happy, confident and invent the things we really need. Like invisibility cloaks and hoverboards.

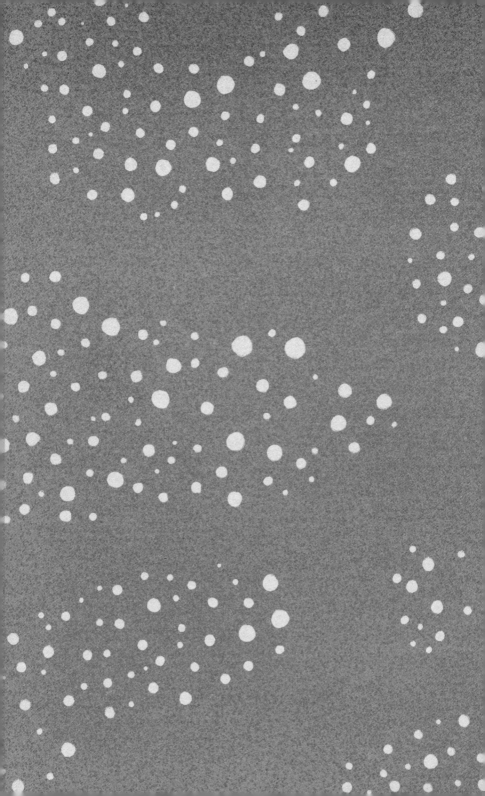

CHAPTER 3

NATURE, NURTURE OR NEITHER?

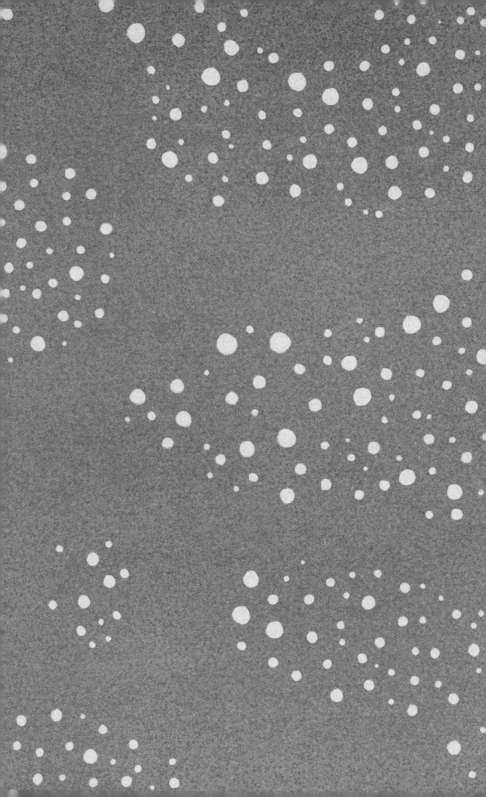

WHY ARE PEOPLE GAY?

'Why are people gay?' This is a question I feel like people are VERY hungry to answer. They love to chat about it. Is it nature (people are born with it) or is it nurture (people become gay)? It's debated in articles, panel discussions, and dinner-table conversations all over the place, both within and outside of the LGBTQ+ community. In this next section we'll look at some of the millions of theories out there about what influences our attractions.

First of all, though, I want to say that in my humble opinion, the answer to this question should be simply,

'WHO CARES?'

I frequently come across articles detailing how scientists are trying to identify and isolate the 'gay gene'. Scientists are ALWAYS trying to find the gay gene, but they never definitively have. (Maybe the stonewashed Levi's George Michael wears in the music video for 'Faith'?) (Get it? Gay jeans. I am a professional comedian.) While we can identify contributing biological factors, there's no definitive proof that same-sex attraction is genetic – we don't know if our sexualities are fixed before or after birth. But man, do scientists keep trying. They're desperate to find that gene!

My first thought when reading those articles is always: Excuse me, scientists ...

WOULD YOU MIND CURING EBOLA?

MAYBE SOLVE GLOBAL WARMING?

SORT OUT AFFORDABLE SPACE TOURISM?

Once you've done that, then perhaps we can focus our energies on the gay gene. Or, even better, we could not? It's not particularly pressing, is it?

If you ask me, William Shakespeare solved this issue when he wrote: 'some are born gay, some achieve gayness, and some have gayness thrust upon them'. That is the quote, isn't it? (It's not.)

I have an anecdote about being asked why I, personally, am not straight. My first boyfriend was a guy called Ethan Peach, when I was about 12 or 13. We were in love. I think we only hung out twice, and on both those occasions we exclusively discussed our favourite flavour of Starburst candy but I'm pretty sure it was love, or the closest to love I could manage at age 13. Ethan once wrote me a letter while he was away at ski camp over the winter. It arrived in the mail and my quivering pubescent hands tore open the Lynx-scented envelope. Inside was the most romantic thing anyone had ever said to me, or has ever said to me since:

Dear Mae,

you are a weird girl,
but I still like you.

Love, Ethan

Anyway Ethan broke up with me ... on speaker-phone while all of his friends were listening and laughing. **I KNOW. RIGHT?!** Anyway I'm over it now (clearly, that's why I'm writing about it in this book) but I was doing an interview recently to promote a live tour and a crazy thing happened. The interviewer said, 'Okay, I'm going to fire ten rapid-fire questions at you' (this isn't the crazy part) 'and you say the first thing that pops into your mind, no hesitation.' He starts firing these questions at me, and they were easy ones to start with: What's your favourite thing about England? (The Spice Girls.) Who's your favourite Spice Girl? (Impossible to choose.) What's your favourite flavour of ice cream? (None, I don't like cold foods and I think ice cream is phlegmy nonsense.) How do you want to die if you could choose your death? (Suffocated gently by all five Spice Girls.)

Then he eventually gets to the final question and fires this one at me:

'WHY DO YOU THINK YOU'RE GAY?'

... Really??? You're throwing that at me as a rapid fire question? I think if I had any time to pontificate I would have gone away and come up with something vaguely intellectual like 'I think labels can be divisive and I personally don't feel the need to identify as anything other than a human being', but ... and this moment will haunt me eternally ... I panicked and blurted out, with no hesitation, 'Maybe Ethan Peach in Grade Seven.'

I wish I could tell you that was the worst of it. Imagine my dismay when the article came out and I read that my response to the question 'Why do you think you're gay?' had been printed as 'Maybe eating a peach in Grade Seven.'

MAYBE EATING A PEACH?

Insane. I called the editor and they refused to adjust my answer ('I'm sorry, that's what you said … that eating a peach might have made you gay'). At first I was horrified, but now I am at peace with the fact that if you google me you will find that I am documented as subscribing to the idea that eating a particularly delicious piece of fruit or produce could turn you. The worst part of the whole thing is that my poor mum has a 'google alert' set up with my name, so any time anything with my name on it appears online she gets a notification email. So my mum got an email with that interview in it, and I got a phone call … 'Is it true? Well, I don't understand that. We gave your brother the same peaches …'

BORN THIS WAY?

The phrase 'born this way' has been adopted by the gay community as a plea for tolerance. You see it on the sides of buses, on stickers, T-shirts and badges – it's super catchy! But without stepping on the toes of some of the amazing charities, etc. that have adopted that slogan, can I just say: I'm not into it. I can't quite get on board. For one thing, if we really look closely at the science it would appear that there's no definitive answer on this, it's certainly not as simple as a gene we can identify. And for another thing, it seems so apologetic! It's like, 'Please, we were born this way! If we could change it, we would!' It sounds like the kind of thing you would say pleadingly before you get punched, not the kind of thing you would shout proudly from a rooftop. It makes it seem like we're only entitled to acceptance if our sexualities are genetically predisposed. And in fact, why do we need to justify our sexualities in this way at all? Heterosexuality isn't subjected to the same rigorous investigation.

I should clarify, just because I'm not a huge fan of the 'born this way' slogan, I'm not saying that I'm on the 'nurture' side of the 'nature vs nurture' debate. I'm of the opinion that sexuality is a complex combination of the two, and that by focusing too much on this question at all we wade into dangerous territory, wasting valuable time that could be spent trying to make the world a better place. Or at least researching how to create holograms of Buffy the Vampire Slayer for the home, or breathalysers for cell phones to prevent us from texting our exes while drunk.

When arguing with someone who fundamentally believes that same-sex sexual relations are a sin (for the record – if you're an LGBTQ+ person you shouldn't feel that you have engage in these conversations if they're damaging to your mental health!), I can see why it's useful to simplify the issue and say, 'Look, I didn't choose this, in the same way that people don't choose their skin colour, so I demand acceptance.' And that is absolutely true. We don't choose who we feel attracted to. But saying we were 'born this way' feels like a dumbing down of a beautiful and complex reality. I disagree with the opinion that sexuality is one of two things: something you're born with, or a conscious choice. 'Choice' is not necessarily the only other alternative to genetics. We don't suddenly wake up one morning and choose who to be attracted to. 'What a beautiful day! Today I would like to fancy Tom Hiddleston despite the fact that it's really not coming naturally.' We choose our actions, not our feelings. And even if we **DID** choose our feelings – who cares? Live your dreams! It's nobody's business but yours who you end up watching Netflix and arguing with. All I'm saying is, you don't have to be 'born this way' for it to be okay. That's not the caveat for being accepted.

I went to a Lady Gaga concert (of course) and it was the Born This Way tour. It was very empowering and wonderful, but there were thousands of people with rainbow 'Born This Way' signs. Signs saying ...

WE'RE ON THE RIGHT TRACK BABY I WAS BORN THIS WAY.

Being a pedantic scrooge on this subject I just wished I had my own sign like 'I don't think we're asking the relevant questions ...' But what are the relevant questions about sexuality, I hear you ask? Well, 'What is everyone's problem?' and 'Can everyone please calm down?' both spring to mind ...

Having said all that, and as much as I hope we're moving towards a place where we don't **HAVE** to discuss sexuality, I'm not denying that the origins of attraction are interesting. Just as **ALL** mysterious matters of the heart and loins are (sorry for saying loins). I guess my feelings about the nature/nurture question are the result of a lifetime of fielding personal and/or uninformed questions about my sexuality from interviewers, friends of friends, confused neighbours, etc. I have a gut reaction. I find it annoying. Why am I being asked when I first knew I was gay by a friend's drunk second cousin who I've just met at a wedding? Why am I being asked whether I'm really bisexual by an interviewer who's meant to be asking about my comedy? I once had someone ask me, 'But really, which do you prefer, women or men?' more than seven times in a row before they finally accepted my answer: 'Neither, it just depends on the person.' When the interview was over he asked passive aggressively why it was so difficult for me to answer a direct question, and I asked him why it was so difficult for him to accept a direct answer, and then we went our separate ways and probably complained about each other to our friends. You don't owe anyone an explanation about your sexuality, and it's not your job to simplify your attractions into terms that others can understand. Actually, the only relevant questions about our sexualities are the ones we ask ourselves, from a place of curiosity and total self-acceptance. Definitely not the ones asked of and about us in a politicised and loaded way, or by radio chat-show hosts who seem to enjoy watching us squirm.

PLAYING HOUSE

Some people want to fit us into boxes to make themselves feel more comfortable. They like to connect the dots in a way that makes sense to them. I have experienced this in such a visceral way most of my adult life. Because my hair is short and I look androgynous, when I meet a dumbo (or even some well-intentioned new friend, if I'm honest) I'm often shocked by the sense of urgency they feel about sorting out in their minds if I'm straight, gay, male, female, trans, nonbinary, whatever. They need to know, but why? So they can decide how to treat me? Of course we ALL prefer things to be simplified and easier to digest. I personally would prefer if the reason I didn't win the junior drama award in Grade

Four, despite my **COMPELLING** portrayal of Charlie Brown, was that there was a simple miscount of the voting ballots. I have to concede, however, that my loss was due to a combination of reasons including but not limited to: I chose to do a British accent for the role, waved at my parents from the stage several times, cried in the final scene, and was up against stiff competition from Victoria Lee who delivered a searing and raw performance as Snoopy. This tendency we have to want to simplify sexuality reminds me of a conversation I had recently …

Every time I go home to Canada, I reconnect with my old school friends, the people I grew up with. Because we only see each other once a year, a lot of those friendships survive solely on the almost ritual recitation of our ever-diminishing collection of old shared memories. 'Remember that time we played spin the bottle and everyone caught pneumonia?' 'Remember when I lied and told everyone that if they came to my tenth birthday party Geri Halliwell would be there handing out puppies?' The last time I was in town, I was reminiscing with an old friend about a game we used to play when we were about eight years old. It was our main pastime on our lunch break for years. Tell me (in your minds) if this sounds familiar. In Canada we called the game 'House', in England I think it's called 'Mums and Dads'? Basically, you get a group of friends and on your lunch break you act out the darkest improvised soap opera. Is this familiar? Usually one really bossy girl instigates and casts the game ('you're the mum, you're the dad, you're the brother, you're the sister in a coma') and then she narrates the rough plot of the scenes you're about to enact. Then you improvise the scenes, and get really involved. Sometimes our storylines evolved over months of lunch breaks! In my memory the plots were always **REALLY** dark. Usually something like: 'Okay, the dad comes home, he's drunk, he smashes a plate and everybody's crying. Then the mum comes home, she says she wants to be a professional singer, nobody in the family supports her, she locks herself in the bathroom and says she wants a divorce ... **EVERYBODY'S** crying. Then we call the police because of the domestic disturbance and the police come round and it turns out the teenage daughter's pregnant with the policeman's baby and the shame of it put her in a coma! **GO**.' And then you act it out! So strange. Anyway, I was reminiscing about these games with my friend, and she said, 'Oh my God, do you remember you always used to play the rebellious teenage son?' I was like 'Yes. Zach. Of course I remember Zach. He rode a motorcycle, smoked cigarettes, and was my greatest ever role.' My friend went on, 'I wonder if that was a sign that you were gonna be gay? Maybe that was a clue that you were going to end up gay!' like she'd suddenly made a breakthrough in a murder case she was investigating.

I just thought to myself, 'If that's true, if the character I played in a game of "House" was a clue about my sexuality, what does that say about Chloe King who **ALWAYS** wanted to be the dog?' (There's **ALWAYS** one girl who's sheepishly mumbling 'Um … can I be the dog?' 'Uh, sure, Chloe. Nobody else wants to be the dog.' She just crawls around your feet while you continue with your game, and you throw her a bone every once in a while and she sits in an imaginary kennel.)

My point is: maybe my dedication to the role of 'Zach' in a pretend childhood game was a foreshadowing of my later sexuality, but we can't pick and choose the things we flag up as predictors. I mean, in that same conversation I patiently reminded my friend that she used to frequently cast herself as the patriarch of our make-believe family – a kind of huge, bulky male mafia boss constantly threatening to assassinate everyone – but she identifies as straight. My friend Simon used to be Princess Jasmine when he and his brothers played 'Aladdin', with teal bikini and all, but he's straight, too.

ANY TIME YOU MAKE A RULE IN YOUR MIND. LIKE 'KIDS WHO PRETEND TO BE THE OPPOSITE GENDER IN SCHOOLYARD GAMES WILL TURN OUT GAY'. YOU'LL FIND A MILLION EXAMPLES WHERE THIS ISN'T THE CASE.

so why worry about it or make sweeping generalisations? As I get into in the next chapter, it's complicated.

ORIGINS OF SEXUALITY

If you are interested in investigating the origins of your own sexuality, there are tons of cool books and studies out there, which all pretty much come to the same scientific conclusion: 'it's complicated'. A combination of biological, environmental and cultural factors – definitely not as simple as 'born this way'. There's loads of evidence that our experiences as babies impact our sexualities. Which makes sense, because when you're an infant and you bond with a parent or caregiver, your brain releases a pleasure chemical called oxytocin. Research suggests that later in life you'll then try to recreate the conditions that initially released that oxytocin when you're looking for sexual partners. Check this out:

TEST ONE

Rats are generally considered to be polygamist animals – aka female rats will literally have sex with any male rat they come in contact with. They're super horny, and totally indiscriminate about who they want to bone. Anything with a pulse. **EXCEPT** get this: in a controlled experiment, some scientists got two groups of female rats which were given daily periods of social play time with either a lemon-scented or almond-scented rat ('almond-scented rat' – the new holiday treat from Cadbury's). They were shocked to discover that when they introduced the female rats into a big group of rats as adults, without fail the rats that had earlier experiences with lemon-scented rats, picked a lemon-scented sexual partner, whereas the rats that had played with almond-scented rats, picked an almond-scented sexual partner.

So the rat's brain would release oxytocin – the pleasure chemical – when she smelled an almond odour for example – but **ONLY** if her early play experiences were with an almond-scented partner.[4] This is in total defiance of everything we think we know about the way rats mate! And has triggered a months long search on my part for an almond-scented cologne.

This supports the idea that our early experiences are not fully formed at birth, as some people would have us believe. No more 'born this way'.

TEST TWO

I love goats and sheep. Goats in particular make me grateful to be alive on the earth. Feeling sad? Go touch a goat. Seriously. Not on the head, though. Did you know that they pee on their own heads when they want to impress each other? Goats appeal to me due to their combination of being very heroic and very embarrassing. There's a petting zoo near my house where I go to hang out with several goats about four times a week. I realise this sounds implausible but I swear the goats recognise me and give me a subtle nod when I arrive. We have an understanding. They know I'm a friend. I have taken many people on first dates to this petting zoo, and the way that they respond to the goats/the goats respond to them is a pretty good indicator of whether I should spend any further time with them. 'This is boring, do you want to get a drink?' = no second date. 'I like the big lumpy one named "Leon", he looks very humble' = marriage.

Anyway, I want to tell you about this verrrry interesting experiment done with goats and sheep that further supports the idea that our sexualities are influenced by our early environment.

So some scientists gave a newborn baby goat to a sheep mum. And they said to the sheep mum 'please raise this goat as if it were your own offspring'. Then they took a newborn baby sheep and gave it to the goat family, as part of a process called 'cross-fostering'. So the goat was raised by sheep, the sheep was raised by goats. Are you with me? Good. Well, guess what. Later in life, the scientists released the goat into a huge field of goats and sheep, and said,

'Go, have sex with whoever you want.' (I don't know if they spoke to it but I like to think they did.) Amazingly, given the choice of having sex with a sheep or a goat, it chose the sheep.[5] The goat preferred sex with sheep! Its early bonding experiences with sheep actually overrode its biological urge to have sex with its own species. That's huge!

These experiments show that sexuality can be influenced by factors other than genes. The truth is, like our personalities, our sexualities are built slowly over time due to an almost impossibly intricate web of factors ranging from hormones in the womb to our social environment later in life. So it's argubaly **NOWHERE** near as simple as 'we're born this way'. (Maybe it's becoming clear I have beef with 'born this way'? I need to get over it.)

Left-wing historian John D'Emilio explained really succinctly why we might be drawn to the simplicity of an idea like 'people are born gay, and sexuality is fixed and unchangeable' and why that way of thinking might be dangerous. He said ...

"Born gay" is an idea with a large constituency, LGBT and otherwise. It's an idea designed to allay the ingrained fears of a homophobic society and the internalized fears of gays, lesbians and bisexuals. What's most amazing to me about the "born gay" phenomenon is that the scientific evidence for it is thin as a reed, yet it doesn't matter. It's an idea with such social utility that one doesn't need much evidence in order to make it attractive and credible.[6]

Basically what John D'Emilio is saying is that the theory that we're 'born gay' is popular in part due to the fact that it makes people (LGBTQ+ and otherwise) comfortable. It's easier to wrap your head round than the more mysterious, and more threatening to some, reality that sexuality is a complicated and dynamic thing, not a trait you're born with. For these reasons 'born gay' has become a conveniently palatable theory with very little scientific evidence to support it, and that's always dangerous.

IT'S COMPLICATED

I've been talking a lot about our sexualities, and I want to clarify that when I say 'our sexualities' I'm not just talking about people who identify under the LGBTQ+ umbrella. **EVERYONE** has a relationship with sexuality! Even your conservative grandparents! Even Theresa May! I feel like that's important to remember. People who identify as straight have sexualities that are as specific and varied and weird as anyone else's, again influenced by their early experiences, etc. None of my female friends who identify as straight are just attracted to 'men'. They all have specific 'types', of course! Likes and dislikes. 'Men with beards', 'French men', 'Emotionally unavailable sociopaths', etc. So where do those likes and dislikes come from?

Nothing happens in a vacuum and our brains are constantly evolving. It's really hard to figure out what is biological and what is influenced by our surroundings. I mean, for example, the fact that in ancient Rome bisexuality was sort of the norm for much of the male population would suggest to me that culture and social structures play a **HUGE** role in sexuality. It's not like there was something in the grapes that turned everyone bi. It was a simple case of everyone being told growing up that men often had sex with men, so that became the social norm.

It's a question open to much debate. How can we ever disentangle our early cultural and environmental influences from our biological predispositions?

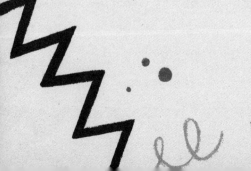

It's almost an unanswerable question. Like ...

'WHY DOES A ROUND PIZZA COME IN A SQUARE BOX?'

or

'IF NOBODY BUYS A TICKET TO A MOVIE. DOES THE CINEMA STILL SHOW IT?'

or

'WHY HAVE I HAD THE SONG "ROXANNE" STUCK IN MY HEAD FOR CLOSE TO NINE YEARS?'

It's equally difficult to figure out what character traits and preferences are biologically linked to gender. Maybe you've heard people talk about 'gender roles'. People often flippantly remark that men are more aggressive than women, or that women are more empathetic than men. Well, it's good to be wary of these generalisations. When you're young and your brain is developing and you're getting a sense of who you are, you learn what behaviours are rewarded and punished by your parents and those around you. One example of this is how we learn gender roles as infants. You pick up on subtle cues from adults about what behaviour is gender 'appropriate' or gender 'inappropriate'. When a little boy picks up a Barbie and everyone around him laughs, or takes it away and replaces it with a truck, he absorbs that. When a little girl is constantly told she is 'beautiful' rather than being told she is intelligent or brave, she absorbs that too and starts to place importance on her appearance. I really think that we are only just beginning to understand gender, and rethink our outdated opinions on masculinity and femininity.

One example of gender socialisation is the experiment done with a baby that was introduced as a male to half of the study subjects, and as a female to the other half. The results are interesting and mildly disturbing! When the study subjects thought the baby was a boy, the baby was percieved as bigger and stronger, and offered (out of a selection of toys) a hammer or a football. When the participants thought the baby was a girl, the baby was offered a doll. The 'girl' baby was also often treated with more nurturance, whereas the 'boy' baby was encouraged to be more active. So people are unconsciously treating us differently from the moment we are born, depending on whether they think we're male or female, and this no doubt affects our behaviour and predispositions.[7]

When it comes to our sexuality, by the time puberty hits, and our attractions begin to appear in a sexual way via 'involuntary blood flow to the genitals' (such an unsexy way of saying 'getting turned on'), so much has already happened. We've absorbed a billion suggestions, prompts and cultural boundaries from the world around us – TV, our parents, etc. We can't control who or what triggers a sexual response. A good way to look at it is: just because we can't 'control' or choose who we're attracted to, does that mean we're 'born this way' or that sexuality is purely biological? No. It's a combination of loads of things. From what we can gather ...

IT'S BOTH NATURE AND NURTURE.

CHAPTER 4

IS EVERYTHING ON A SPECTRUM?

THE
SEXUALITY
SPRECTRUM

'Is Everything On A Spectrum?' is a question I'm hearing everywhere and something I'd like to dive into here, unpicking the idea and discovering whether things are binary when it comes to love, sex and dating. Human beings have a real tendency to sort things into 'binary' categories, that is – categories of two distinct and opposing values, for example 'black/white'. It helps us make sense of the world. Our brains like to oversimplify complex ideas by breaking them down into these opposing extremes. We find it comforting to think in terms of good/evil, gay/straight, liberal/conservative, male/female, happy/sad ... but if we look closely at these things, are they really as simple as we think? Is it possible that in looking at ideas in these terms we are oversimplifying them, just to make them easier to compute?

Let's take 'good and evil'. Is anyone pure evil, or pure good? Pretty rarely, I'd say. None of the great heroes in history or literature would be half as compelling as they are, or capture our imaginations the way they do, if they were **JUST** good and heroic. The greatest heroes are flawed (Batman would be a terrible dinner guest, so broody and humourless; 'I have expensive gadgets on my belt and I am definitely **NOT** Bruce Wayne' isn't the most stimulating table chat), and every iconic villain has some redeeming humanity (Darth Vader ultimately loves his son and just wants him to join the dark side, for example. Or Ursula the sea witch is very evil but also **INCREDIBLY SEXY**). People have layers of complexity, that's what makes them human.

How about 'happy and sad'? Are we ever just happy? Or just sad? Or are we always a heady combo of emotions? (Right now for instance, I'm a bit happy about the sandwich I'm eating because it has nice bread with VERY nice seeds on it, a bit anxious about global warming, a bit horny because Zayn Malik is on the radio, a bit ill ...) Do we really have to be just one thing? I was born and raised in Canada, but my dad is British and I've lived in England for eight years. So what am I? A Brit or a Canuck? In England, people say I'm deeply Canadian (earnest, find sarcasm stressful, heavily into folk music, eat a lot of donuts), but I've been here for so long that when I go back to Canada my Canadian friends say I now sound British, and they bully me by throwing pine cones at me when I'm trying to build my igloos and harvest my maple syrup! Bloody unfair, eh?

Sexuality is similarly amorphous, I think. Although lots of people do fit into the two ends of the sexuality spectrum (I'm definitely not denying that some people are completely straight and some people are completely gay), for the most part, in my opinion the population doesn't actually fall neatly into the two extremes of '100 per cent homosexual' and '100 per cent heterosexual'. Let me explain!

SEXUAL SCALES

There are so many shades of grey in between the two extremes, and you may have heard people throwing around the term 'human sexuality spectrum' as an alternative way of thinking when it comes to gender and sexuality. This is the way we're headed, I think, in the way we discuss sexuality, and it refers to the idea that sexuality exists on a continuum that accounts for every variation of human sexuality/identity without necessarily labelling or defining all of them. It's the idea that your sexuality can change throughout your life (or in my case, hour by hour) and might not exist definitively inside a strict label. I **LOVE** this idea, and it's one that I've found to be true in my own life. Why does my sexuality have to be a fixed thing instead of an evolving vibe in a given moment? Right now in this exact moment my sexuality is, exclusively, Jamie Dornan dressed like a train conductor, because of a YouTube video I just watched. But in a minute, it might change to Jamie Dornan dressed like an aloof millionaire ... and eventually I will close YouTube and my sexuality will change again, hopefully into something unrelated to Jamie Dornan because that's becoming a problem. Life is a rich tapestry.

People have been talking about the 'spectrum of sexuality' ever since a famous sexologist (horny job alert) called Alfred Kinsey invented 'the Kinsey Scale' in 1948.[8] This is a scale that runs from 0 to 6, from exclusively heterosexual (0) to exclusively homosexual (6) with an additional category of X which represents people with 'no-socio-sexual contacts or reactions'.

0   1   2   3   4   5   6   X

But as we've evolved in our thinking about sexuality, even this has become too rigid and inadequate in describing all the different types of human attraction and identity. If you google it, you can actually take a quiz online to see where you fall on the Kinsey Scale but you may find, like I did, that it's a little over-simple and falls short of expressing exactly how you feel. Quizzes that claim to be able to assess the crevices of your soul with a few snappy questions usually do fall short, I find. The other day I did a Buzzfeed quiz which told me that, based on my McDonald's order and favourite types of cheese, I am a 'Chandler/Rachel' combo (from *Friends*). I take great exception to this. I am clearly a Ross/Joey with Monica rising. I've also been told definitively by the J. K. Rowling 'Sorting Hat' quiz on the internet, that I am a member of the Hogwarts House 'Ravenclaw'. I could write an entire chapter of this book explaining the breadth and scope of the Slytherin and Gryffindor qualities I possess, but my publishers have called this 'unwelcome' and 'a bit mad'. While we're talking about HP, though, wouldn't you say that Harry Potter himself – the poster boy of Gryffindor house – falls somewhere in between Gryffindor and Slytherin? Even the sorting hat wasn't sure which house to sort him into. Harry made a choice to be placed in Gryffindor, I would say largely influenced by cultural, social and family expectations that he **SHOULD** be a Gryffindor. Just like we are prone to do when we give our sexuality a strict label, Harry chose the house to which he felt he was most culturally suited, but in doing so he chose to mute some aspects of his complex identity. I'm just saying I wouldn't be surprised to run into Harry at a Slytherin club after hours, and there's no shame in that.

I'M NOT GAY, BUT ...

I've been using the term 'sexuality' a lot. Another term I'm going to throw at you is 'orientation', which is another way of saying 'who you're attracted to'. Looking at the origins of orientation tends to bring up big academic and philosophical questions. What is 'orientation'? Is it just what physically turns us on, aka sends blood involuntarily to our genitals (am I making everybody want to never ever have sex by using that phrase?)? Or is it more than that – is it a cultural identity and a conscious choice?

I asked Dr Meg-John Barker to weigh in on the question of what the difference between sexuality and orientation is and I liked their answer ...

'They often get used interchangeably, but sexuality refers to the whole of our sexual way of being, and sexual orientation tends to refer just to the gender of the people we're attracted to (who we are 'oriented' towards). It's an important issue because activists and academics alike have pointed out that reducing sexuality to sexual orientation – as our culture tends to do – is bad for everyone. There are so many dimensions to our sexualities beyond which gender(s) we're attracted to, such as what level of desire we have, what kinds of bodies we fancy, what fantasies we find hot, what roles we like to take in sex, what physical sensations we enjoy, how many people we're sexuality attracted to, etc.'

Interesting, right? Amazingly, studies have shown that men and women who identify clearly and happily as one orientation (like 'homosexual' or 'heterosexual') are still aroused by pornography or sexual images that don't match what they've said they're turned on by. For example, men and women who identify as straight often show clear physical indicators of arousal when watching same-sex pornography.[9] There was even a study which showed that straight women became aroused watching lesbian bonobo apes going at it in the wild.[10] Surely that doesn't mean that these women are attracted to bonobo apes, right? Our minds and bodies are so complex. Several of my female friends who identify as straight tell me they frequently think about women while they masturbate. To me, all this supports my belief that it's crazy to say we have to fit into one of three distinct categories of orientation – gay, straight and bi – those categories don't begin to cover the infinite complexities of our sexualities. Later on we'll be talking about labelling sexuality, and the problems that can present too.

SO, there can be a big gap between how people identify and what actually arouses them. And the

things that do arouse us can be different to how we
might express our desires in public – for instance a
bisexual person might like men and women but only
end up dating women. Are you with me? Basically,
it's all crazy, it's all over the place, and it's pretty
mysterious.

What do we use to define our orientation? Is it simply
what we think about when we're masturbating? If
so then I think a lot of us would be single forever
because we'd be swiping through dating apps trying to
find some faceless body or random obscure situation
that turns us on – a minotaur with the face of your
old school teacher, Tom Hanks in *Apollo 13*, whatever
floats your boat. I used to masturbate thinking about
the repulsive evil old wizard Jafar from *Aladdin*
when I was about 13. He just kept popping into my
brain unbidden, as iconic villains often do. I swear,
I wasn't thinking about him on purpose, he would
just appear in my mind's eye wearing his ragged old
cloak, wielding his hypnotising staff and trying to trap
me in an hourglass full of sand and it seemed like
too much effort to ask him to leave. Does that mean
that's my sexual identity? Jafarsexual? Have you ever

had a sexual dream about a family member, or worse, Donald Trump? That doesn't mean that's who you're attracted to in your waking life.

WE'RE COMPLICATED, OKAY?! OLD CRAGGY JAFAR ACTUALLY HAD A KIND OF ENTICINGLY MISCHIEVOUS ENERGY, OKAY??

One really old and famous statistic is that one in ten people are gay.[11] Ten per cent of the population. Well I have a theory that 10 per cent of the population are completely **STRAIGHT**. It's not hard to imagine that 10 per cent are gay, 10 per cent are straight, and 80 per cent fall somewhere in the middle. I mean, our closest genetic relatives the bonobo apes are pretty bisexual, so isn't it possible that a significant percentage of humans are too, or at least have had fantasies or experiences with both genders? I know a lot of people who, by definition, are bisexual, but prefer to identify as either gay or straight because they say it's 'easier'. The result of this is that bisexual people have had a harder time fostering a community and often feel invisible or 'erased', because people often identify their orientation according to who they are currently dating rather than who they are attracted to, which is often people of all genders.

People get stressed about labels. I wish I had a pound for every man or woman who's approached me after a stand-up show (usually one where I've discussed this kind of subject matter) and told me something that begins 'I'm not gay, but ...' They conspiratorially take me aside, sometimes when their girlfriend or boyfriend is in the bathroom, and tell me in hushed frantic whispers that they've had some same-sex experience at university, or that they fantasise about some celebrity who's the same sex as them ('I'm not gay but I keep dreaming Jason Statham is massaging my testicles, and I like it. What does that mean?' is a real quote), or even that they once had a secret gay relationship. I get anxious emails from people all the time who want to tell me that, although they're straight, they've had gay experiences or feelings. The main question they want to ask is whether I think that means they're gay. It's weird how rarely it occurs to people that they might be bisexual, and it's even rarer that they think actually, it doesn't matter 'what' they are.

So I don't believe that only 10 per cent of people are gay. I think many or even most of us fall somewhere along the spectrum of sexuality, rather than at either end of it. I do, however, remember hearing that statistic at times in my childhood and feeling like part of a small minority rather than part of the vast, horny human race. Although even then, I couldn't wrap my head around that being a bad thing. If it is true that 10 per cent of the population are gay, I remember thinking 'Aren't things that are rare usually very valuable?!' Diamonds, for instance. (I read recently on the *Guardian* website that astronomers have found a planet that's riddled with diamonds. Loads of them. So maybe they'll find a planet that's 'riddled with gay' one day.) Or blue lobsters – very rare. Did you know that one out of every two million lobsters is a beautiful bright blue? They're so valuable, if you're a lobster fisherman and you catch a blue lobster you're like 'Oh my God. What a glorious day for me and my family.' I feel like the gay thing should be like that. If parents get a 'gay' kid, it should be an 'Oh my God **YESSSS**' moment – like finding a four-leaf clover. If a friend of yours ever has a gay kid, I recommend you respond exactly as if they have found a four-leaf clover. 'Wow! I can't believe you got one! You're so lucky! Hold on to it ... You should laminate it and keep it in your wallet.' Or something along those lines.

GENDER

It's not just the 'sexuality spectrum' either, the 'gender spectrum' is another term we're starting to hear more of too. Are we really simply either male or female? What about an estimated 1 in 2000 people who are 'intersex' (born with any of several variations in sex characteristics including chromosomes, gonads, sex hormones or genitals)? What about the trans population? (In the simplest terms, transgender means a person whose sense of personal identity and gender does not correspond with their birth sex.) Or people who identify as nonbinary? (Nonbinary is a catch-all term for gender identities that are not exclusively masculine or feminine but exist outside the gender binary of male and female.) You hear people talking about the 'gender spectrum' these days more and more – everybody's whispering about it down the pub ('Packet of Mini Cheddars and a nuanced opinion on masculinity, would ya Tom?'). Let's have a go at explaining it ...

So your sex is to do with your biology and physical characteristics (having been born with a female reproductive system, genes and physical characteristics, I was assigned female at birth), and your sexuality is who you're attracted to physically and romantically. But gender is much more complex, as it can be on a spectrum from 'entirely male' to 'entirely female', and there are people that feel they fit in anywhere in between the two or with neither. Gender is about which set of characteristics you identify with the most, what you deeply feel, and can change more easily. Still with me? Good, because there is a spectrum of gender identity and to make sense of it, I am going to use a Disney analogy:

So at one end of the spectrum you have **EXTREME** masculinity: ultra hyper masculinity which, to me, is **GASTON** from Disney's *Beauty and the Beast*. Remember him? Giant red triangle with a ponytail? Carried a big gun? Three fainting ladies followed him around the town square?

Then, at the other end of the spectrum, you have extreme femininity, which is like Belle from *Beauty and the Beast*. (Who has Stockholm syndrome, by the way. Why don't we talk about that ever, but it's hands-down the darkest Disney plot of all time. She falls in love with her kidnapper, a giant dog-man. Talk about Beast-iality. But she's still an excellent role model I guess, because she ... likes books? Can read?) And then dead-centre in the middle of the spectrum you have the French candlestick! You have Lumière! I really relate to that guy, I think I'm the candlestick. He's the best, he's so welcoming. He wants everyone to 'be his guest' and 'put his service to the test' which is coincidentally what I say whenever I'm about to have sex with anyone.

I think most of us sit between the two extremes of macho Gaston or super-swish Belle; gender-wise most of us are closer to one of the pieces of crockery in the Beast's castle, probably some kind of gravy boat, or fork.

We're living in exciting times, and more and more options are becoming available to people in terms of how they want to define/not define their gender. My relationship with my own gender identity is even shifting, now that new language is available to me. I often wonder if I was growing up now whether I would opt to use gender neutral pronouns or identify as nonbinary. I have no idea. I know that I don't feel entirely comfortable saying I'm a 'woman', that word has never sat right with me, because I often feel like a Backstreet Boy and have spent my life feeling more connected to and identifying with a 'masculine energy' (whatever that means), but I definitely don't feel like a man either, and often feel deeply connected to being a girl. Anyway I'm thinking about it, and trying not to be stressed about it. I'll keep you posted.

NAKED CHRISTMAS

Our experience of our own gender identity is much more complicated than what's between our legs, and it's impacted by cultural messages and all kinds of other things.

I was lucky that my parents were hyper-vigilant about gender stereotypes when I was growing up. I was talking to them about it recently and a terrifying revelation was made. I said, 'Being so aware of gender stereotypes must have made it tricky at Christmas because, especially in the 90s, a lot of the presents you'd normally get for kids were quite gender specific, like you'd get the same toy and it's pink for a girl/blue for a boy.' And my dad calmly said, 'Well no that wasn't a problem for us because you didn't want toys until you were eleven.' My initial reaction was 'What?!' and then they said, 'Don't you remember? Until you were eleven you only wanted one thing for Christmas' ... Then the memories came flooding back and I felt the blood draining from my face ... 'All you wanted every Christmas was permission to be completely naked for the entire day.' **WHAT WAS I THINKING?** Until age eleven I was an aspiring nudist. Eleven is too old! Your limbs are so long at that age! What's more, we used to fly over to England for Christmas every year to visit my grandmother. My poor grandmother, she must have dreaded Christmas morning, when her weird spider monkey granddaughter would descend the staircase '... this is my Christmas gift ... for myself and all of my family ...'

The worst part is that the photos they produced to prove to me that this was true are photographs of the **FORMAL** family Christmas dinner, where it was not just my immediate family but the extended family – cousins and second cousins who I only saw once a year. Not only is everyone else at the table fully clothed but they're dressed UP! They've put more layers on if anything – the kids are wearing little suits and bow ties and I'm there draped across the chairs … 'More gravy anyone? … Pass the Brussels sprouts, cousin …'

ANYWAY, my parents were strongly opposed to the more traditional ideas of what constitutes 'feminine' or 'masculine' behaviour, which is lucky for me because they didn't bat an eyelid when they found me flexing my biceps in the mirror and desperately trying to memorise John Travolta's dance moves from *Saturday Night Fever* at the age of ten. Having short hair and dressing the way I do, I often get people asking me online what gender pronouns I use, or assuming I'm not a girl. Ever since I was a kid, dressed in my finest waistcoat and trousers, people on the street, in toilets, on buses, literally everywhere you might encounter the general public, have asked me whether I'm a girl or a boy. It doesn't bother me much having to correct people and tell them that I'm a girl. After all, I've had to do it at least once a week for my *entire life*. It does, however, always strike me as strange how narrow people's idea of what a girl should look like is. Nor does it ever cease to amaze me how stressed out people get about any ambiguity around gender. How urgently they need to know what genitals someone has, and how entitled they feel to demand that information.

Just recently I received this (hopefully well-meaning?) tweet:

'I tried to show a friend a @theMaeMartin sketch and she just screamed

"IS IT A BOY OR IS IT A GIRL?!"

for five minutes straight.'

I mean …. If you ask me, it's time to get some new friends who are less easily panicked. Then maybe you'll also have some better anecdotes to tweet at me!

My dad used to take me to the gym with him when I was about nine years old. I would look forward to it all week, and pretend to use the machines while he worked out, mimicking what he did, waiting for him to go in the pool with me. There was always a moment of anxiety, though, when we'd part ways afterwards and head to our separate changerooms. I'd get sceptical 'looks' from women by the lockers because I was on my own, with a boy's haircut, usually with my towel tied around my waist because that was how I felt most comfortable, instead of wearing it tucked under my armpits around my flat chest. Ferris Bueller wears his towel around his waist when he comes out of the shower in *Ferris Bueller's Day Off*, and he was my hero at the time, so I couldn't understand why I shouldn't wear my towel the way he does.

One day I was getting ready to take a shower, maybe flexing my biceps in the mirror, and an irate middle-aged woman approached me. Her face was an extraordinary shade of red and a vein was popping out of her neck. 'This is the **WOMEN'S** changeroom. It's not FOR you.' She thundered. 'I'm a girl,' I replied, shaky from receiving her palpable rage. 'WHERE are your parents? **GET OUT. PLEASE!**' she bellowed. I was in shock, bundled up my clothes, threw them on in a toilet stall, and went to the lobby to wait for my dad. I remember sitting there, the sticky chlorine I hadn't been able to wash off drying on my skin, looking at the doors to the men's changeroom on my left, and the women's changeroom on the right, and feeling I wasn't welcome in either. If you ever see anyone angrily policing someone else's gender, please step in and tell them to worry about their blood pressure before they worry about other people's genitals.

The extremes of masculinity and femininity which all advertising (perfumes, make-up, cars, deodorant) would have us believe should be our ultimate goals and get us constantly laid, are pretty rarely achieved. In fact, they're not meant to be. They're ideals that are designed for us to fall short of, which produces anxiety, which then makes us spend more money!

Resist! Flex your biceps, girls! Move your hips, boys!
Do some kind of deep lunge, everyone else!

Wouldn't it be nice to live in a gender-neutral
environment, and let nature take its course in terms
of our interests and behaviours? I don't doubt that the
way I was brought up has affected my attitude to this
stuff. I've always dated women and men at least partly
because I never believed that gender defines a person
– other qualities make them attractive or interesting.
I'm going to talk about that in the next chapter, if
you're interested. Hey thanks for reading my book, by
the way, if you're still with me.

MY TOP 5 TURN-ONS

A fun surprise in my life has been that as I get older, I feel like gender is becoming less and less important in terms of what I'm looking for in the person I want to end up with. Not just because I'm getting increasingly desperate, I swear. Other, more specific things are moving up the list in terms of what I'm into, and those things have very little to do with someone's genitalia. Here are my Top 5 Turn-ons. Maybe you can relate to some of them ... maybe not.

1.

First of all: winking. A
confident, unexpected *wink*
to me either says 'we're going to have
sex' or maybe 'we just had sex. Great job,
congrats'. (I've never received a post-sex wink
actually, but I'd be chuffed.) There's a guy who
works at the coffee shop by my house, and he's
an extremely prolific winker. He'll sometimes
wink at me four or five times over the course
of making one coffee. By the time I get
the drink I'm like 'I'm spent … I'll
see you tomorrow.'

2.

Somebody diving into the
water with excellent form. Picture
this: a placid Canadian lake, maybe at a
... summer camp in the 90s ... the sun is rising,
maybe there's a lone moose in the shallows, wading
through the reeds, and somebody runs to the end of a
wooden pier and they dive off the end with such excellent
form, there's barely even a splash when they go in the
water. And maybe you're swimming in the lake and they
dive **OVER YOU**. Hot? If you're not sold yet, what
about this: you're swimming in the lake, they run to
the end of the pier, dive over you, and as they're
flying over your head they look down,
make eye contact, and **WINK**.
FIT. right?

3.

Somebody driving a diesel-
powered speedboat. I can trace exactly
why I'm into this – I used to go to summer
camp as a child, quintessential North American
summer camp with a lake and bonfires and cabins. I
was a gangly, prepubescent spider monkey (my limbs
were **SO LONG**) with braces and acne ... Anyway the job of
driving the waterskiing boat was given to the alpha-female
camp counsellor, who would be some tanned athletic
blonde in a hoodie with a ponytail and hoop earrings
driving the boat so confidently (careful to avoid the
moose) wearing Oakley sunglasses and her name
was Katie. (Yeah, okay, this one's less vague
and more specific.)

4.

Somebody buying me a
drink when I haven't requested one. I
like the presumption of it! I even like it when
they **PRESUME** what I'm drinking. Have you seen
Titanic? Do you remember that scene in *Titanic*, when
they're having a posh lunch, and Caledon Hockley, the
villain of the film, orders on behalf of his fiancée **Rose
DeWitt Bukater** without checking with her? It's very rude
and presumptuous. 'We'll both have the lamb, rare, with
very little mint sauce.' **EVERYONE** in the cinema was
tutting away like 'what a villain!!' and I was ... into
it. 'Okay, I'll have the lamb if you think I'd
enjoy the lamb! So sue me!'

5.

And finally: being woken
up in the morning when I'm sleeping
in my bunk-bed by a girl in a hoodie
who's just got out of the shower so
she smells like shampoo and she's like
'We've got to get up and go to the dining
hall for breakfast, then we have to go to
our respective activities and I'll drive
the waterski boat. Hi, I'm Katie.'

(If you're reading this and your name is Katie and you were definitely the camp counsellor at my summer camp – hello. I don't know what you're like now, but you were very very undeniably cool when you were about 18. I'm sorry that I frequently told you and all the other staff members at the camp that I was 'scared' of you. You weren't scary. You were super nice. I think I was just having feelings in my stomach I hadn't felt before, and the closest comparable feeling they resembled was abject terror, so that's what I thought the issue was.)

OTHER RUNNERS UP ON MY TURN-ON LIST

PEOPLE USING MY NAME.
This might seem broad and potentially problematic given how frequently people generally address other people using their names, but whenever someone unexpectedly uses my name (e.g. 'How's your day been, Mae?') I become a puddle on the floor. It's inconvenient. ('Do you have the time, Mae? ... Mae? Oh. She's liquefied, drained into a gutter, and now she lives in the sewer among the Truly Horny. That's a shame.')

BUFFY THE VAMPIRE SLAYER.
She's so selfless, she knows karate, and she could protect me from myself and others.

BRITISH PEOPLE IMITATING MY ACCENT BACK AT ME.
I guess I like the attention, and the fact that they always make me sound like Alicia Silverstone in *Clueless*.

NICE HANDS.
I perv on people's hands the way other people perv on cleavage or jean bulges. On dates, I've been known to sit, with a creepy vacant look in my eyes, mesmerised by the way someone's holding a drink.

BEING IN THE PASSENGER SEAT OF A CAR WHEN ANYONE IS DRIVING.
I think that has to do with not being in control of my own destination. And maybe something to do with the seatbelt?

PEOPLE MAKING FUN OF ME.
Someone once told me that I look like an IKEA lamp, that my legs are sticks, and that when I sleep I look like a plank of wood. Nothing has ever turned me on more. I don't know why.

THE DANCING GIRLS IN THE MUSICAL *CHICAGO*.
They're so dedicated, motivated and talented, and they've committed cold-blooded musical murder.

FATAL ATTRACTION

Nobody is attracted to an entire demographic – for instance, a gay man is not attracted to ALL men – and, as evidenced by that not-even-exhaustive list of my personal turn-ons, attraction is very complicated … It's also linked up with early experiences (as we saw with the rat ladies), pheromones, conscious and unconscious thoughts (as we saw with my unconscious desire to bone Jafar). But I'm pretty sure that everyone has a 'Katie from camp' – that is, someone from around puberty who you're just weirdly drawn to, even in a non-sexual way, someone you put on a pedestal and are obsessed with. Right? Not just me? (Hello?) And often these early crushes transcend gender and are more about authority, or confidence, or whatever.

When I was a kid I was obsessed with basically anyone who knew all the lyrics to 'Gangsta's Paradise'. I also had an all-consuming passion for the iconic diva Bette Midler. Actually, can I talk about Bette for a minute?

I **LOVE** Bette Midler. She's vivacious, she's outrageous, and as a singer, dancer and actor, she's a triple threat. I saw the movie *Hocus Pocus* when I was six and I became incurably devoted to her. If you've never seen *Hocus Pocus*, first of all I feel sorry for you, and secondly it's a 90s Disney film about three witches who come back from the dead to terrorise the town of Salem. Bette plays the most powerful of the three witches, naturally. Picture me as an impressionable six-year-old:

BOWL CUT AND THE ONE OUTFIT THAT I ALWAYS WORE WHICH CONSISTED OF: A FORMAL MEN'S BLOUSE (CRISPLY IRONED, BUTTONED TO THE TOP), RED TARTAN TROUSERS, LEATHER SHOES AND THEN MY PRIZED GARMENT – A SUEDE WAISTCOAT.

It was a hand-me-down from my older brother that I got given on my birthday. My parents wrapped it, which was annoying. Have you ever unwrapped a hand-me-down waistcoat on your birthday? 'Oh I've seen this. Many times. For years.' But after the initial disappointment wore off and I reluctantly tried it on, my life changed. It was like when Peter Parker puts on the spider suit for the first time – man oh man did I feel confident in that thing. I looked at my reflection in the mirror and thought 'Okay, now we're cooking with gas. Things around here are gonna change. There's a new king in town.' I wore it every day for about four years, it was the uniform of my childhood. It was definitely a weird look, I think I looked like a kind of Victorian serf, or a Charles Dickens character, bowing obsequiously as I left the room. Imagine a spider monkey humbly bowing, limbs trailing the ground, as they back slowly out of the room declaring 'Dinner is served, my liege ...'

I went to see *Hocus Pocus* roughly ten times in cinemas. My wonderful parents would drive me, occasionally they'd wait in the foyer and I'd go in by myself, with so many snacks, bowing in my suede waistcoat to the ticket guy ('My usual seat please, my liege') ... Bette was

the thing that kept bringing me back to *Hocus Pocus*.
I loved her. I saw the world through a lens of Bette
Midler. If it was a sunny day I'd wake up and think:

I WONDER WHAT
BETTE IS DOING ON THIS
BEAUTIFUL MORNING.
WHAT IS SHE WEARING?
WHAT IS SHE THINKING?
IS SHE THINKING
OF ME?'

I didn't realise at the time that I had a crush on Bette Midler. I didn't know that it was a sexual thing at all, but I did know enough to know that it was a **PRIVATE** thing, sort of a special thought that was mine only, and that, if possible, I preferred to be physically alone when I thought about her. I was very open about that. After dinner with my parents I'd politely fold my napkin and rise from the table. 'Thank you for a lovely meal, but if you don't mind I'd like to retire to my bedroom at this time, to dedicate some time to thinking about Bette.'

My room was a shrine to Bette. The walls were covered in photos, including my most treasured one which was a semi-nude of her covered in rose petals. Yup, just a 6-year-old girl staring at a 45-year-old naked woman covered in rose petals. Looking back, how did I even procure this vast collection of photos? I was six. I had no disposable income to speak of, so my parents must have been helping me source these images? Their supportiveness never ceases to amaze me.

I had my first sex dream about Bette Midler. Well, I say sex dream, but no sex actually occurred, there was just sort of a ... vibe? I don't know if you remember your first vibey dream, where you woke up feeling slightly guilty and confused, desperate to get back to whatever vibey place you were just inhabiting in your subconscious? In my dream the witches had kidnapped me so that they could steal my soul to make them eternally young (that's the plot of *Hocus Pocus*, I wasn't a creative genius). The thing was, there was a real vibe going on between me and the witches. It felt as though they were going to steal my soul, yes, but then maybe we were all going to hook up, ferociously. I could never get back to 'complete' the dream and it's one of the great tragedies of my life.

FLUIDITY

So, if sexuality is complicated and isn't binary, what is it? There is a word I'm very excited about at the moment that you may have heard floating around, and that's 'fluidity'. It reflects the trend towards people not feeling the need to ever identify as one thing or another. It's the idea that sexuality isn't a fixed thing, but a dynamic one that can change over time and therefore you don't have to label yourself as anything.

People have also been speaking more and more about fluidity of all types, including 'gender fluidity', which refers not to your sexuality but to your gender identity.

Here are just a few examples of celebrities who are jumping on board the 'fluidity' train:

JOSH HUTCHERSON

In an interview with *Out* magazine, Josh Hutcherson discussed his fluid sexuality, how he's not sure what the future will hold and he's fine with that:

'Maybe I could say right now I'm 100% straight ... But who knows? In a f–king year, I could meet a guy and be like, Whoa, I'm attracted to this person ... I've met guys all the time that I'm like, Damn, that's a good-looking guy, you know?' [12]

Josh Hutcherson's stance on sexuality is pretty familiar to me, having grown up in Toronto, Canada, which is a kind of beacon of fluid sexuality. Many of my ostensibly straight friends, who have never had same-sex experiences or relationships at all, refuse to identify as 'straight' or 'heterosexual'. I just want to quickly shout out my best friend Gaby Leith, who is a **CELEB TO ME**, and said something once that stuck with me:

'Why would I say I'm straight just because those are the experiences I've had so far? Who's asking me to define it and why? Even though I might be straight now, saying so just means that if at some point I meet a woman, I'll have to "come out". I don't want to be put in a box.'

MILEY CYRUS

Miley Cyrus has said she's both sexually and gender fluid. She told *Paper* magazine about realising she couldn't label her sexuality at a young age, saying:

'I remember telling [my mom] I admire women in a different way. And she asked me what that meant. And I said, I love them. I love them like I love boys.'

She also touched upon her gender identity, adding:

'I don't relate to being boy or girl, and I don't have to have my partner relate to boy or girl.' [12]

RUBY ROSE

Ruby Rose discussed her gender fluidity in a 2015 interview with *Elle*, saying:

'Gender fluidity is not really feeling like you're at one end of the spectrum or the other.

For the most part, I definitely don't identify as any gender. I'm not a guy; I don't really feel like a woman, but obviously I was born one. So, I'm somewhere in the middle, which – in my perfect imagination – is like having the best of both sexes. I have a lot of characteristics that would normally be present in a guy and then less that would be present in a woman. But then sometimes I'll put on a skirt.' [13]

KE$HA

Back in 2013, Kesha dished on her sexual fluidity, telling *Seventeen*:

'I don't love just men. I love people. It's not about a gender. It's just about the spirit that exudes from that other person you're with ... I wouldn't say I'm gay or straight — I don't like labeling things anyway. I just like people.' [14]

ELLY JACKSON

La Roux's Elly Jackson said to the *Guardian* in 2010 that she's both gender and sexually fluid, saying:

'I don't have a sexuality. I don't feel like I'm female or male. I don't belong to the gay or straight society, if there is such a thing. I feel like I'm capable of falling in love with other people. I'm not saying I'm bisexual, I'm just sexual!' [15]

DEMI LOVATO

In an interview with *Complex* magazine, Demi Lovato had this to say about sexuality:

'By the way, love is fluid. Humans are humans, and when you connect with somebody on a spiritual level it doesn't matter.' [16]

CHAPTER 5

NEVER READ
THE LABEL

HEY I'M SINGLE

Previously we looked at sexuality being a spectrum and at the increasing number of celebrities that are refusing to define their sexuality and gender or label themselves. In this part I'd like to take a closer look at the way we label our sexualities, and the potential benefits and pitfalls of having a word or term to identify yourself with.

I've been single for the past year or so – properly single for the first time since I was a teenager. And it's absolutely ... fine. I'm catching up on a lot of important things. Yesterday, for instance, I watched 17 crucial videos of baby goats who had been trained to dance. One was wearing a hat! It's been a really productive few months in that sense. I've even been catching up on my reading. (Well, I've been reading my ex's Facebook page. Does that count? That's all I read. I read it like it's a thriller – like it's *Gone Girl* and I need to know the plot twist.)

Still, I'm enjoying being single, working my way through various dating apps with the dogged determination of a marathon runner; jaw clenched, drenched in sweat, full of resolute persistence. Farting loudly alone in my bed. **NEVER** sharing my Pringles. Never being forced to endure watching some new 'talked about' series when I can happily watch repeats of 90s sitcoms that warm my heart. Truly, though, despite these perks I am a relationship person. I'm romantic, and I like focusing on one person at a time. Like, if I'm a dating marathon runner the only reason I entered the marathon in the first place is for the moment at the end when I cross the finish line, and someone throws their arms around me and tells me I can rest. I'd kind of like to invent my own app that's specifically tailored to my needs. It would be for bisexual comedians over 30. Probably it would end up being hundreds of photos of my own face, as

I'd be the only member. I'd gently caress my phone, swiping right endlessly. The app would be activated only by my tears – you have to cry a single tear on to the home button of your iPhone to unlock it. **JUST KIDDING I'M FINE GUYS**. I swear. I would quite like to date myself, though. Not out of narcissism but out of anxiety: I would text myself back **SO FAST**. I'd never even have to see the grey ellipsis that appears when someone's typing. It would just be an instant response.

> **Me: Hey.**

> **Me2: HEY.**

> **Me: Love you.**

Me2: LOVE YOU TOO.

Me: How are you?

Me2: SCARED.

Me: Why?

Me2: I dunno.

Me: Same.

This year, I've been mixing it up and dating men as well as women. It's pretty crazy how shocked my friends initially were by that. I mean sure, that's partly because of the current climate – with the whole #metoo movement it seems like a pretty weird time to be suddenly 'getting into men'. Besides that, though, nobody **EVER** believes that I'm attracted to men, I suppose because I have short hair. I'm aware I look like the blond one from One Direction. (Who am I kidding, calling him 'the blond one' like I don't know his name. It's Niall Horan. He's a Virgo. From Ireland. And he's very important to me as both my doppelgänger and crush.)

I immediately downloaded a dating app as soon as I was single (well, slightly before I was single), and on this app you can set your settings to attract the demographic of people you want to date.* So, you put the age you want to attract (I put 20–700 ... you want to cast a wide net), and you select the gender you want to attract as well. So, I set my settings to match with men **AND** women (if there had been a nonbinary/intersex/transgender category I would have clicked that too) and I was really surprised by

*By the way, you can't access dating apps unless you're over 18 and if you're not, I wouldn't recommend going on them – especially when there's so many other ways to meet people.

how shocked my friends were when I told them this. They were really thrown. My young, cool, progressive friends! I guess they had only ever known me to date women and it didn't compute. Some of them weren't just shocked, they were borderline annoyed about it, as if I'd somehow betrayed their trust! They were like 'What? ... No ... but ... your hair ... you lied ... You lied with your hair.' It's always a shock to me how narrow our ideas of what a heterosexual person 'should' look like, versus what a gay person 'should' look like are. Really, is our sexuality as flimsy as a haircut?

My whole life people have told me that I'm gay. They have no problem informing me of this, regardless of my opinion on the matter.

'You're gay'

'Your face is gay'

'Your hair's gay'

'You dress gay'

'You talk gay'

'You walk gay'

Even the men that I go on dates with often challenge my assertion that I'm 'into men'. I once went on a date with an acquaintance of mine, a comedian. We'd had a few drinks and we started making out (I'm kind of a legend) and out of nowhere he just stopped and said, 'God, this is really crazy for me ...' 'Why?' I said, 'What do you mean?' 'It's just crazy making out with you cause ... I'm not even gay!' I patiently explained to him that as I am a girl, and he is a boy, this situation could not be any more heterosexual, and he shrugged apologetically. 'Sorry, you know what I mean ...' (I didn't) 'I've just never been on a date with a lesbian before!' I couldn't believe it. Infuriating! What did he think I was doing, field research? A lesbian undercover on a date with a man to find out how the other side lives? What was doubly annoying was that prior to us kissing we had been having a 20-minute conversation about the band the Red Hot Chili Peppers. I'd been nodding gravely, 'Yes, Flea is an excellent bassist, although I don't know their newer albums very well ...' After the revelation that he thought I was a lesbian I thought, 'So ... you thought I **WANTED** to be talking about the Red Hot Chili Peppers? For **TWENTY**

MINUTES? NO! I'm putting the time in because I am trying to have sex with you.'

At times, I've identified as gay out of convenience. When you've been in a relationship with a woman for five years, spend a lot of time in a wonderful lesbian community, and you 'look like a lesbian', it seems pointless to assert that you have, in fact, been in love with men before. It starts a conversation you might not be in the mood to have. But it's not a good feeling to have a label imposed on you that erases a good chunk of your identity. This is a common problem for people who are attracted to more than one gender. You (and your sexuality) become defined by the gender of your current partner.

Even one of my best friends in England reeled when I told him I was dating men again. 'Really?! You want to date men?' 'Yeah, if you don't mind ...?' His response was 'I'm sorry, I guess I can't picture it. I can't picture you having sex with a man.' My response to that is always: first of all, please refrain from picturing me having sex at all. And secondly: Really? You can't picture it? That's so sad for you, how crappy is your imagination? I am capable of picturing anything I want. At any time. That's the joy of having an imagination. Try it! Right now, I'm picturing that all five Spice Girls are circling my house on broomsticks singing '2 Become 1'. It's wild, Geri is literally going nuts. My friend went on to politely reiterate a question I've been asked a great deal in my life: 'If you don't mind me asking, what are you? I've always assumed you were a lesbian, so what are you? How do you identify?' Strangely, I genuinely don't have an answer to that question! I mean I guess if I was pressed I'd say I'm bi, or 'queer' but … why am I being pressed, you know? I want to make it clear that just because I'm reluctant to label my sexuality, it doesn't mean that I'm 'confused', or obfuscating, or being coy. It also doesn't mean that I'm not massively proud to be part of the LGBTQ+ community. I also recognise the importance of being vocal about that, and visible.

Many of the significant relationships in my life have been with women who have never been with women before. I don't know why that is, it just seems to have worked out that way. More often than not, after a period of adjustment, this doesn't present much of a problem, but occasionally it does. Usually where the anxiety comes from is around the idea of suddenly being asked to adopt a 'label'. My ex had this experience. She suddenly found herself in love with a woman, and it was really new to her, and she worried that people would suddenly assume that she was a lesbian, and that she had been in the closet her whole life, which wasn't the case. It was a real source of tension in our relationship, her anxiety about being 'mis-labelled', and her reluctance to even identify as bisexual.

I was constantly trying to reassure her that it was the 21st century, that she didn't have to label herself in any way and that people wouldn't be constantly assuming she was a lesbian just because she was with a girl. The problem was – that kept happening. One day, a friend of ours called Patsy Wilson was introducing us to her mum, who we'd never met before. And she was like 'Oh Mum, these are my lesbian friends I told you about.' My ex visibly flinched at being referred to as a lesbian. I wanted to say to Patsy, 'Oh really? It's the 21st century and we're still introducing people based on who they're having sex with? Well, in that case let me re-introduce you to your mum: Mrs Wilson, you know Patsy, she mostly dates guys that look exactly like her dad. We all think it's really weird but ... you raised her!' In my fantasy I then cheerfully skip away into the sunset, leaving them in my wake.

It is easy for me to get frustrated with all the stress my exes have around being with a woman and how people would see that. It can be infuriating and depressing, it makes me feel like people are ashamed of me, and anyone who's been in a similar situation will understand how deeply rattling to one's corn-cob core that can be! No matter how many times someone says, 'this is my issue, it has nothing to do with you, I think you're amazing', you still internalise the part that says, 'don't touch me in public'. I've had relationships where people would come round and she'd introduce me as her roommate. I'd be there, half naked ... 'Oh hello ... I'm the weird roommate ...'

In retrospect, though, I think I sometimes forgot, or could be insensitive to, the fact that not everyone had the experience I did, growing up. I pretty much won the lottery in terms of environments to grow up in as a queer kid, ensconced in a very rare liberal utopia. I know that is not the reality for many.

IT'S HARD OUT THERE.

GAY MAE

I want to talk about my parents Wendy and James again. Here we go. Wherever you're sitting reading this book, just pause and give Wendy and James a quick round of applause. Mum and Dad, if you're reading this, give yourselves a quick pat on the back. As I've already mentioned, I remember my mum saying, 'You're going to grow up, you'll meet a man, or a woman, and fall in love, and no matter what it'll be great ... I mean, you're going to have to work on your personality a bit if you want to meet a **GOOD** man or a woman ...'

Remember, I never had to come out to my parents. I always brought home girls and boys and they never asked me about it. I mean, genuinely, the only coming out experience I had with them was coming out as a comedian. And that was traumatic. I was like 'I'm a comedian' and they sat with their heads in their hands like '... maybe it's just a phase?!' But maybe it's because I never had to come out to them, that my sexuality never felt like a huge part of my identity ... it felt very incidental and casual. And that attitude has probably reinforced the opinion I currently hold that the way we label or don't label our sexualities, the people we fall in love with, etc., doesn't necessarily have to comprise a huge part of our cultural identity. It's not the most interesting thing about us.

It wasn't until I left home that I realised my sexuality was even going to be a thing that would get flagged up, something people would notice and use to define me. I remember the first article ever written about my comedy – it was a review of a stand-up show I did. I was 16 years old, and when the review came out it was titled:

'INTRODUCING: GAY MAE'.

I wasn't annoyed at the time at all! I was actually really excited! I remember thinking

'GREAT, I'M GAY MAE!'

When you're young and still figuring out who you are, it can be really exciting and positive to have an identity you can wrap yourself in. I remember thinking

'PERFECT. THAT'S WHO I AM, SORTED.'

It felt different and like I belonged. I was being booked to perform at fun gay events and being embraced by this amazing community. At the time I didn't focus much on the fact that I wasn't strictly 'gay' but was actually attracted to all types of people, and it didn't bother me to be pigeon-holed. In fact, I was very pleased about it. I was skipping around town. People would ask me, 'Do you have the time?' and I'd reply, 'Oh no, I'm sorry, I'm gay.' 'Do you take milk in your coffee?' 'No thank you. I'm gay.' I was quite smug about it! I leaned into Gay Mae!

It was an interesting mental shift, though, because it was also the first time I realised to my shock that I was now part of a marginalised community. Somebody said to me, 'You're so lucky you're growing up in such a tolerant city' (Toronto is well known to be a very 'tolerant city') and … up until that point I thought I WAS the city. Suddenly I found myself living in a city that was 'tolerating' me. I hope from the bottom of my heart that in the not-too-distant future we're able to erase the expression 'tolerance' from the vocabulary we use in discussion around LGBTQ+ communities. We should tolerate inconveniences or distasteful annoyances, not people. Like I tolerate the fact that some neighbours have been loudly divorcing for the past six months and that I know the intimate details of their marital problems. He's emotionally distant and she's too aggressive, and I tolerate that. Although, if my neighbours are reading this: guys – get out of the garden when you're talking about how you've ruined each other's lives, I'm trying to sunbathe. The LGBTQ+ community can and should expect more than tolerance from the world. It's a world that we have enriched and created along with everyone else.

So now that I'm single (did I mention that?) and people are asking me questions about who I want to date (now that I am, just one more time, quite single) it's really the first time I've had a moment to pause and think 'Am I still Gay Mae?' Sometimes I feel like super-gay Mae. When I'm watching Sarah Michelle Gellar as Buffy the Vampire Slayer single-handedly save the world from being sucked into a vampire-ridden hell dimension, for instance. Could not feel gayer than when I'm watching that occur. Other times I feel like super-straight Mae: when Leonardo DiCaprio finally won an Oscar for *The Revenant*, for instance,

I turned to my friend with tears in my eyes and said, 'That's my man up there' and spent the rest of the night in bed furiously masturbating. (Do not invite me to your Oscar party!) If I'm being honest, though, 99 per cent of the time I don't feel like 'gay Mae' or 'straight Mae' or 'bi Mae', I'm just thinking about what sandwich I want to have for lunch (cheese toastie, every time).

What I believe we should reject is being labelled by other people, without our consent. I don't like that people look at me and make assumptions, assume things about my gender or who I sleep with, and I don't like feeling that who I choose to sleep with is any more a part of who I am than it is for someone who lives a heterosexual life. For instance, up until very recently, in almost everything in the media about me or my comedy, my name has this prefix attached of 'lesbian comedian'. It's frustrating. First of all, I don't identify that way: listen to like five minutes of my stand-up and you'd know I'm all over the place. Secondly, 'lesbian' or 'gay' is not a genre of comedy, and it's sometimes treated that way. I'm a comedian. I talk about childhood, relationships and my personal experience of being a human, just like every other comedian. But I've often been told by club promoters or comedy festival bookers, 'Sorry, there's no room on the bill, we already have a lesbian comedian on'. When they say 'the bill' they mean the list of comedians booked to perform, and nine times out of ten that bill is populated almost exclusively by straight white men. It sucks that I'm jostling for the one spot allocated for 'diversity'. I've also been asked by promoters to veer away from talking about 'gay stuff' on stage. Does that mean I'm not allowed to talk about my love life at all? If a man talks about his girlfriend he's not labelled a 'straight comedian', but if I talk about mine it's politicised and suddenly I'm doing 'gay material' when I'm just trying to explain how infuriating it is when my ex drunk texts me 'You up?'

ON THE OTHER HAND

So yes, I believe very strongly in a future where we don't have to label our sexualities or be defined by them. Where we're free to date who we want without having to answer questions about it or 'come out', where basically a book like this would be *totally unnecessary* because sexuality is such a non-issue. It's occasionally tricky for me to express this without sounding like I'm somehow ashamed of who I am. As though the reason I don't want to label my sexuality is that I'm uncomfortable with the label itself or want to distance myself from the LGBTQ+ community. That's not the case. That community (along with the comedy community) is the community I grew up in. I want to make it clear that I'm not saying that there should be no 'gay culture'. I grew up in the cradle of Toronto's gay community, drag queens and older lesbians surrounding me like warm amniotic fluid letting me blossom (I mean, did I blossom? Does anyone blossom?) into exactly the person I wanted to be. It was only yesterday that the LGBTQ+ community had to fight tooth and nail to be able to wave a flag of pride and clearly identify themselves without fear of arrest and persecution. That fight is still raging, legal rights are still tenuous, and if we're complacent we could easily slip back to the Dark Ages. When I say 'there's no need for labels' I suppose what I really mean is there's no need for other people to impose labels upon us. There's no need for us to be defined by who we are attracted to. There's no need for us to feel pressure to clarify our sexual identities if we don't want to, or feel stuck in that label once we have it. Our labels should be helpful to us, and they shouldn't make us feel like we only have a place on the fringe, or that our stories aren't welcome into big old mainstream life and culture.

The LGBTQ+ community remains vitally important – a lifeline to people who are often rejected by their own families and local communities. I want the LGBTQ+ and gay culture in general to flourish forever, but not as a reaction to oppression. Only as a self-labelled, self-styled entity, free of the rigidity that comes from being put on the defensive for generations. And I'm not naive. I do recognise why visibility is still an incredibly powerful thing. It's still illegal in 72 countries to be gay, punishable by death in 8, so we're definitely still in a place where it's crucial that we're able to wave that banner, to say you stand with and are part of that community. The labels and language that we have around sexuality are an important tool in discussing oppression. How can we discuss oppression if we don't have a language for it? But I do sometimes imagine a future where these labels are obsolete, and we can just get on with it.

BI ERASURE

As you may have gathered by now because this book is clearly a thirst trap designed to find me a spouse(s), I am attracted to men, women, and everyone in between, both, or beyond. And it's funny how reluctant people still are to believe that anyone can be attracted to more than one gender. That seems archaic, I know, but it's remarkable how often I have this conversation with friends, even gay friends, who say, 'Yeah it's not really a thing, you'll pick one, you'll settle on which one you like more.' If you have short hair like me, abhor wearing dresses and you mostly date girls, and you say, 'Oh I'm attracted to that man over there,' people are like, 'Prove it Ellen DeGeneres. We'll believe it when we see it.' If you have long hair and you mostly date boys and you're like 'I could see myself with a woman one day,' people think you're doing it for attention because it's trendy, or it's a phase, or you want to turn on boys ... If you're a **BOY** and you say you're bisexual, people are like 'Absolutely not. No way.' They think your sexuality's like a payment plan ... Like

'BI NOW ... GAY LATER...'

I googled the official definition of 'bisexuality' and was really surprised by how broad it is. This is Robyn Ochs's definition, which is widely accepted in the queer community:

'I call myself bisexual because I acknowledge that I have in myself the potential to be attracted – romantically and/or sexually – to people of more than one sex and/or gender, not necessarily at the same time, not necessarily in the same way, and not necessarily to the same degree.' [17]

It's so broad! And I think people from both camps would probably fit into that category but are reluctant because they feel pressure to have a clearer social and cultural identity, which the heterosexual community and the homosexual community both have. It's also very frustrating having to prove that you exist all the time, to sceptical members of both communities. I just went on Google and typed in 'bisexual' and the first recommendation that came up in the search bar was 'do bisexuals exist?' – ridiculous.

POSTIVES AND NEGATIVES TO LABELS

I asked Dr Meg-John Barker about the benefits and disadvantages of labelling our sexualities.

What are the benefits of labelling your sexuality?

Labelling your sexuality opens up the possibility of finding a community of other people who experience their sexualities in similar ways, as well as making it easier to be clear to possible sexual partners about what your sexual attractions and desires are (if you have them – always important to remember asexual folk here). Labelling sexualities has also been an important part of fighting for LGBTQ+ and other sexual rights historically. It can be hard – in our identity focused culture – to gain visibility or rights without a label. The proliferation of labels for a range of sexual and asexual identities can also be really helpful for people who are trying to figure out their sexuality – giving them options to explore.

What are the disadvantages of labelling your sexuality?

Labelling your sexuality can make you feel fixed in that way – as if it isn't okay if that label stops fitting so well. Also, there are a limited range of labels. What if you end up choosing one that doesn't really capture or communicate your experience? This is particularly a problem given that the most common labels are mostly about what gender you're attracted to (straight, bi, gay, etc.) and that might not be the most important feature of your sexuality at all.

Finally, many of the labels have a history of being seen as more or less normal in wider culture so it's not just an easy thing to pick the label that fits best for you. For many people it's still too dangerous to identify under certain labels as they may carry the risk of violence, discrimination, or being ostracised from the family/community.

Dr Barker's comment about 'labels are mostly about what gender you're attracted to (...) and that might not be the most important feature of your sexuality at all' rang particularly true for me. The labels of gay and straight and bi seem to fall short of explaining what it is about a person that I'm attracted to. They're focused on the gender of the person, whereas I'm more focused on their bank balance. Just kidding – I'm more focused on their energy, sense of humor, and if they smell nice and are good at diving into water.

Labels can be quite narrow and can bulldoze over the nuances of something so dynamic, complex and individual. Sexuality is so interesting, why are we dumbing it down?! For instance, I used to have a fantasy when I was about 11 that I was Steven Tyler from Aerosmith (who incidentally identifies as gender fluid), and I would stand in front of the mirror at home with my shirt billowing open, being very male, lip syncing all the words to the crowd ... but in the fantasy, the whole auditorium was filled with screaming hysterical crying men with boners. So, I'm just saying, as I keep saying throughout this book (thanks again for reading this book) – we're very unique and individual. Wouldn't it be interesting if we could experiment with eliminating the terms? What would happen if you just eliminated the terms heterosexuality and homosexuality, and called it all 'human sexuality'? It's all under that umbrella anyway ... and it's SO much easier to get away with being 'homophobic' than it is to get away with being 'humanphobic'. You'd never leave your house, you'd be petrified all the time! 'They're everywhere! Gross! Humans!'

US AND THEM

The minute you label a group of people you make
it a lot easier to create an 'us and them' situation,
It becomes much easier to see yourself as separate
when really there is no us and them, it's just **US**.

If we start to see sexuality as an US thing, not as a
niche issue for the people concerned to get behind,
it suddenly becomes very accessible. What could
be more universal than sexuality? We've all got
one. It's so easy for people to say 'oh there's that
kooky community again' / 'good fences make good
neighbours' etc. But LGBTQ+ rights help us all! You
don't have to be gay to be called a 'fag' in high school.
As far as I could tell at school 'fag' was an umbrella
insult encompassing short kids, loners with the
wrong colour hoodie, and boys who were too good

at drawing. Also you don't have to be gay to have gay kids, and all of a sudden, it's totally personal and relevant to you. You don't have to be queer to feel the immense pressure to look or behave in a way that matches the gender stereotypes of your genitals. You don't even **HAVE** to be gay to, at some point in your life, meet someone of the same sex and fall in love. You could be 50 years old and meet someone, and fall in love unexpectedly, and suddenly find that the fight for equality has a profound relevance in your life that you could never have predicted. What I'm saying is ...

YOU DON'T HAVE TO BE GAY TO BE GAY.

(Should I make merchandise?!)

So, what should we call ourselves? How should we label ourselves? I guess the answer is incredibly vague because really, it's 'whatever we want'. We should call ourselves whatever we want, disregard the things people label us without our consent, and we should stop asking people WHAT they are and focus more on WHO they are. The vital thing is that we tell each other, tell our kids, our friends, our ex-girlfriends, that if they don't want to, they don't have to call themselves anything at all.

In general, the more we can eliminate this sense of 'otherness', the stronger a society and sense of unity we're going to have as a species! And this doesn't mean we can't celebrate our differences, it just means we don't have to be defined by them.

CHAPTER 6

COMING OUT
(AND GOING BACK IN)

WHEN DID YOU COME OUT?

The number one question I get asked in interviews is, 'When did you come out?' People ask me that before they even ask me if I'm gay, they just assume. That question of 'When did you come out?' reflects an assumption that I was ever 'in', and as I'll explain in this chapter – I've always been 'out', whatever that means.

There's a lot of debate around whether public figures have a responsibility to be open about their sexualities. On the one hand, it is undeniably **SO** helpful for young LGBTQ+ people who are coming up against bigotry at home or out in the world to have visible role models who are unashamed about who they are. But on the other hand, there's a kind of rabid appetite for salacious details of people's sex lives that makes me uncomfortable. I think the reason a great many celebrities don't 'come out' is that they know they'll then have to field an onslaught of personal and invasive questions, and their sexuality will suddenly begin to define them and overshadow other aspects of their work and career. I definitely understand the reluctance, and I think it's an entirely personal decision. Instead of bullying people for not coming out, let's fix the system that demands the information, and rework it so that people can be open without getting 'Gay Mae-ed' against their will.

The truth is, though, the more we see people speaking openly and casually about their sexualities the more we normalise and demystify it, and that's **SO** valuable. I can't possibly overstate how important it was to me as a teenager to hear Ellen DeGeneres come out. I know it might be difficult now to imagine a time when Ellen was not openly gay (I mean, she wears those three-piece suits so well) but believe it or not, when

I was a kid Ellen was a heterosexual comedic actress starring in a sitcom called *Ellen* about, among other things, trying to find a boyfriend. It was a monumental moment in television history when Ellen's character 'Ellen' came out to her therapist (played by Oprah Winfrey ... I mean **IMAGINE** if Oprah Winfrey was your therapist. You'd be superhuman). '**HOORAY!**' I shouted at my TV and then 'Oh ... damn' when the headlines started rolling in ...

'ELLEN'S SITCOM CANCELLED...'

'Thousands protest Ellen's lesbianism'

'Pundits predict Ellen could never front a wildly successful and dance-positive talk show'.

Her sitcom was axed almost straight away amid outrage at Ellen's openness. The world wasn't ready for it then, but times have changed ... a bit! I was so inspired recently to read a quote from Amandla Stenberg, a young actress (from *The Hunger Games* among other things) who recently came out. She was asked the question:

'WHAT DO YOU LOVE ABOUT BEING GAY?'

This, first of all, is a refreshingly positive angle for an interview question. She responded, so much more eloquently than I ever could:

'I'm grateful for how being gay has afforded me this ability to experience and understand love and sex, and therefore life, in an expansive and infinite way. The continual process of unlearning heteronormativity and internalised homophobia can be difficult, but one of the biggest blessings lies in the magic that comes from having to understand love outside the confines of learned heterosexual roles ... Once I was able to rid myself of those parameters, I found myself in a deep well of unbounded and untouchable love free from the dominion of patriarchy. My sexuality is not a byproduct of my past experiences with men, who I have loved, but rather a part of myself I was born with and love deeply.' [18]

I'm aware I was the luckiest kernel of corn in the land to never have my early romantic experiences tainted by the stress of 'coming out' to my family or friends. I guess the reason I never had to come out to my parents is that they never **ASSUMED** I was straight. That seems so basic to me, but we do sort of assume that all babies are straight, which is crazy because they're **BABIES**. We assume they are straight and then if they're not straight then they have to tell us! They have to break the news like 'Um *cough* excuse me ... These ubiquitous TV advertisements of nuclear heterosexual families aren't resonating with me.'

Embarrassingly, even I catch myself making these same assumptions all the time. My friend has a two-year-old niece and we were all hanging out the other day. They'd just got back from one of those baby drum circles ... you know, the places where babies bang objects and roll around in a circle and the parents sit behind them, dewy-eyed, whispering 'They are **SO** talented ...' while the eccentric woman who runs the group skips around in a circle tapping them all with a wand and blowing bubbles, wearing many layers of skirts and 25 scarves (she never seems to have children of her own ...). Anyway, they had just got back from one of these baby drum circles and I heard myself saying to this two-year-old girl, I guess to make the other adults laugh, 'So, do you have a boyfriend yet? Who's your boyfriend at the baby drum circle?' **EW.** what am I doing?! She could turn out to be the gayest kid in the world, but we make these assumptions all the time. We're basically cutting the umbilical cord and planning the hen night at the same time ... 'Aw, she's precious, so delicate. Pre-order the feather boas and the male strippers for twenty-five years from now.'

Even coming out as a teenager is a bit perplexing to me. What other preference do you have to declare around puberty? You wouldn't ask a 13-year-old what kind of music they're going to listen to for the **REST OF THEIR LIFE**. If you'd asked me I would have said 'Coldplay until I die. Nothing but Coldplay until the day I expire, destroy all other music, I have no use for it.' And oh boy would I have been annoyed if I'd been expected to stand by that declaration when some of Coldplay's later, crappier albums came out.
It's also bizarre to have to field an onslaught of

questions about desire when you're only just figuring out that whole part of yourself and are meant to have the freedom to explore. I have a friend who came out to her parents and the first of a million questions they asked was 'What turned you off men? What was the straw that broke the camel's back that turned you off men?' If I said my favourite food was Italian food, you wouldn't ask me 'What turned you off curry – did you get burned by curry? What was the samosa that broke the camel's back? When did you first realise you were a fan of Italian food, what were the early signs in your childhood that you might one day like Italian food? So, what, are you going to start dressing Italian now? Hanging out at Italian bars?' It's like, 'No! I just found an Italian restaurant I'm really into at the moment. They do a mean linguine.' (I wanted to call this book *Mean Linguine*, but they wouldn't let me. I'll just add it to the list of potential band names.)

I just hate that the pressure of answering an onslaught of questions could take the excitement out of dating, for anyone. My last five relationships have been with women who have never dated women before (yes, I should spend more time in gay bars). I saw first-hand how the stress of explaining to people that they'd fallen in love with a girl took the joy out of those early days of dating. I remember my ex telling me she had been chatting to everyone at work about a date we'd been on, the way anyone would, when her boss, who had been eavesdropping, snapped at her, 'So you're a lesbian now?' She was taken aback. 'Well, no. I just met a girl I like.' 'Well I don't know why you need to tell everyone about it and rub it in everyone's face.' She was crushed and embarrassed. She had just been chatting about a new relationship, and suddenly she was made to feel like she was making a huge statement about herself. When I picked her up from work she felt like she was making a political statement by being seen with me, and she shouldn't have had to feel that way.

GAY PANIC

I asked a friend of mine recently why he waited until his mid-20s to tell his male friends that he was gay, even though he was pretty certain of it himself from the age of about 17. 'I didn't want my friends suddenly thinking I had a crush on them. They were my oldest friends, we'd showered together, wrestled, shared the same bed and stuff, I didn't want them looking back and worrying I'd been perving them the whole time, which I hadn't.' I mean – if this is truly what those boys would have assumed, then new friends are in order. I hear this a lot and it drives me insane. This might seem obvious and ridiculous to you but you'd be amazed how often people make this assumption – 'Oh my God, you're gay? Awesome, I'm so comfortable with that! Um, does this mean you have a crush on me?' **YOU WISH. DUMBO!** (By the way, does this book make it seem like I'm just constantly annoyed? I'm not, I swear.)

BEING A GAY MAN DOES NOT MEAN THAT YOU ARE ATTRACTED TO ALL MEN AND BEING A LESBIAN DOES NOT MEAN THAT YOU ARE ATTRACTED TO ALL WOMEN. JUST LIKE BEING STRAIGHT DOESN'T MEAN YOU'RE EQUALLY AND UNIFORMLY ATTRACTED TO AN ENTIRE GENDER AND BEING BISEXUAL DOESN'T MEAN YOU'RE ATTRACTED TO ALL HUMANS.

Once, my friend Rachel introduced me to a female friend of hers. We all had a drink, and later that night Rachel told me that when I'd gone to the bathroom her friend had said, 'I think Mae has a crush on me.' What could I possibly have done to give her the impression that I had a crush on her? Made eye contact? Had I unintentionally given her the impression that I found her lengthy dissection of exorbitant housing prices in London titillating? The assumption was that, as a girl who likes girls, I must be overflowing with sexual frustration at having a conversation with an attractive straight woman. I think it's an assumption that happens a lot – that gay people are attracted to **EVERYONE** of their sex. The reality is, she was the only one who'd been thinking about sex. I was thinking about whether I'll ever get on the property ladder. (Not likely! Please tell people to buy this book!) It's a phenomenon often called 'gay panic', the fear that any gay person is going to be overwhelmingly attracted to you just because you're of the same sex as them, and this panic results in a lot of unnecessary hysteria and bigotry. Honestly, most people are very picky. Most people have specific types. I once ended a date because the other person declared that the only talented member of the Beatles was Ringo. A deal breaker for me, no offence to Sir Richard Starkey.

FREQUENTLY ASKED ANNOYING QUESTIONS

If you're unsure about something related to sexuality, the best thing you can do is ask questions! It's so refreshing when someone takes the time to ask, before they take a wild stab in the dark.

'WHAT PRONOUNS DO YOU PREFER?'

'HOW CAN I BE A BETTER ALLY?'

'HOW DO YOU IDENTIFY?'

'CAN YOU EXPLAIN TO ME WHAT THIS TERM MEANS?'

are all examples of respectful and useful questions that most people would be happy to field – in fact I bet they'd be chuffed that you're unruffled enough, and interested enough, to ask.

'BUT WHAT IF I OFFEND SOMEONE BY ASKING THE WRONG QUESTION?'

I hear you shout. Here's a handy tip – exercise basic rules of social etiquette. Before you ask the question, ask yourself

'IS THIS A QUESTION THAT WOULD BE BETTER SUITED FOR GOOGLE?'

EXAMPLE SCENARIO:

You're at a party with friends, there's a momentary lull in the conversation, and someone smiles kindly at you:

> *'I've always wanted to ask you, would you mind describing your genitals to me in detail?'*

You'd be so weirded out, right? Not the most comfortable situation, but it's one that many transgender people find themselves in frequently – being put on the spot in public situations fielding the most personal questions. I can't speak for everyone but as a rule I think genitals are very much only the business of the person they're attached to.

In almost every relationship I've been in with a woman I've been asked, 'Who's the man in the relationship?' I always try to explain: we're both women. Truly – no man involved in the equation. Incredulous and undeterred, the questioner presses on. 'No, you know what I mean. Who represents the man?' Honestly, it's like asking a vegeterian, 'Which part of this salad represents the pork chop?' None of it. It's a salad literally entirely made of vegetables. What they really want to know is 'Which vegetable wears the strap-on penis?' and the answer is, in my sex life at least, pretty much all the vegetables sometimes wear them. Even the long-haired vegetables. And when they do, it's very exciting for the short-haired vegetables. It's like a national holiday.

A female friend of mine recently dated a woman for the first time. After they broke up, 99 per cent of her friend's first reactions were: 'So who are you going to date now, boys or girls?' 'So are you gay now?' 'So when you go on dating apps are you going to set your settings to women or men?' – use my handy 'common social etiquette' rule and it will quickly become clear that the more appropriate questions in this scenario would have been: 'How are you feeling?' or 'Are you okay?'

What I'm saying is, it's possible that

IF YOU'RE NOT 100 PER CENT STRAIGHT YOU MAY HAVE TO FIELD A LOT OF DUMB QUESTIONS.

They could be from friends, strangers, enemies, snakes, whatever. They could come from a well-meaning place, or an antagonistic place. An important thing to remember is – you don't have to answer

to anyone. I've been fielding these questions my whole life and often in the heat of the moment and depending on your mood it's hard to come up with a pithy, eviscerating response. Here are some examples of questions I've been asked and responses I wish I'd thought of:

Q: When did you first realise you were gay?

A: When did you first realise you were straight?

Q: Does this mean you have a crush on me?

A: YOU WISH, DUMBO!

Q: How do lesbians have sex?

A: Google it.

Q: How do gay men have sex?

A: Google it.

Q: *Is lesbian sex 'real' sex?*

A: Yes.

Q: *Do you sometimes get turned on by your own body?*

A: Do you sometimes get scared by your own stupidity?

Q: *Who pays for stuff on dates?*

A: Did you know that we live in the 21st century?

Q: *Will you be my gay best friend?*

A: My best friends earn that title through years of listening to me complain about things that are entirely within my control, and lending me money. See how you get on and let's re-evaluate in a decade.

Q: *Why do gay people always have to TALK about being gay?*

A: If you had fewer legal rights and were constantly under threat of violence and discrimination, you'd talk about it too.

Q: *Why aren't civil partnerships enough for gay people? Why do you NEED gay marriage?*

A: Because separate isn't equal. Equality means having the same rights and opportunities as everyone else.

Q: *If two women are having sex using a strap on, doesn't that mean they'd rather have a real penis?*

A: No, it means they'd rather have a silicon penis attached to a woman.

A HAPPY PLACE

If my kids end up being gay I don't want them to have to come out to me. I think we should create an environment for our kids where they don't have to. If my son comes home one day with a boyfriend I don't want to ask all those probing and difficult questions, like 'What does this mean? Are you gay now?' I just want to ask the *important* questions like, 'How much money do his parents make?' Because I'll be broke. I know I will. My kids are bound to have annoying, expensive hobbies like the oboe.

I don't think everyone has a responsibility to speak about their sexuality if they're in a public sphere. Just as nobody is obligated to divulge any other details about their private life. I do think, however, that when we go beyond a simple omission in the interest of privacy and start to actively deny or lie about our sexualities then we reinforce the idea that it's something to be ashamed of, and that's a very dangerous and sad thing. I also think that, as we're still living in a time when LGBTQ+ youth are almost five times as likely to have attempted suicide compared to heterosexual youth, we can't underestimate the value of representation and chatting about this stuff openly. What I **HOPE** is that we're moving towards a happy place where the responsibility isn't on celebrities to declare their sexualities and deal with the consequences, but on the world at large to create an environment of total acceptance and indifference, so it's not necessary to 'come out' at all.

Social progress is being made everywhere you look these days, even though, in the Trump era, it may sometimes seem like we're slipping backwards. It's been really heartening this past couple of years to see that feminism has got massive! It's all over social media. It's very exciting. I'm noticing for the first time that a lot of my male friends are really getting engaged in it, starting to post and share articles, to get angry on behalf of their female friends, and to feel involved in the issue. Similarly, with the racist attacks that have been perpetrated by the police in the States, I'm noticing for the first time how universally appalled people are finally starting to be, people of all races are getting involved in the 'Black Lives Matter' movement. It's a great shift, but I've at times found it disheartening that I often don't see my straight friends posting and sharing articles about LGBTQ+ rights with the same enthusiasm. I posted an article the other day about trans rights, and my best friend said to me later, 'That was a really interesting article.' 'Oh, you should share it, you have tons of Facebook friends ...,' I replied. Suddenly he got nervous and mumbly. 'Eeeerrrm ... I went to an all-boys' school. I have those guys on Facebook, and if I start posting tons of gay articles, they're going to think I'm secretly gay.' I mean, I just don't think that's how it works. If I post 'Black Lives Matter' material, people don't think I'm secretly black! These are human rights issues and relevant to everyone.

Probably, like my parents who don't encounter homophobia in their social sphere or hearts and so are loathe to think it exists, that friend is unaware of how valuable a bit of vocal support from an ally can be. If you are straight and don't encounter 'micro aggressions' every day (aggressive stares, questions, etc.), or don't experience what it's like to exist outside the binary heteronormative world we navigate, it's hard to fully grasp how exhausting it can be.

I told that same friend about something that happened to me a few weeks ago to illustrate that these things are still relevant and pressing. I went to a pub in Islington recently with some friends. Islington! London! Zone 2! It was my friend's birthday and he'd reserved a little area for us. Two things happened in very quick succession when we arrived in this pub. First of all, I went to pee. As I often do. If you know me you'll know that sometimes, I gotta pee. In the toilet there was a group of girls on a hen night fixing their make-up in the mirrors, and they were **WASTED**, a cacophony of screaming and laughter filled the room. I went in and instantly tensed up, as I've had bad encounters with groups like that before.

As I shuffled to the loo they did a double take, the way people have been doing my whole life in public toilets because of my short hair. They erupted into protest: 'WOT? THIS IS THE GIRLS TOILET! WHAT ARE YOU DOING? THIS IS THE GIRLS TOILET.' I mumbled, 'Oh I'm so sorry I AM a girl. I'm very sorry' and went into the stall. I could hear them whispering outside and then one of them knocked on the stall door politely and said, 'Excuse me, ARE YOU A LESBIAN?' and then they all started CHANTING 'dyke' at me. They were singing it like a football chant. I encounter mild homophobia a fair amount, but the level of this aggression freaked me right out. I got stage fright and was too scared to pee – which is RARE for me, I can ALWAYS pee! I'm peeing right now as I write this! I left the bathroom. They came out and sat at a nearby table and were still laughing and looking at me. One was taking photos of me on her phone. I didn't want to bring the mood of my friend's birthday gathering down, and I was worried if I told anyone what had happened I'd start crying (I cry very easily in life. I've been known to cry at insurance adverts on TV, or the beauty of a passing dachshund) so I just sat quietly. But I wanted to feel safe I guess, so

I put my arm around my friend Bertram Alfred Peek, and put my head on his shoulder ... and as soon as I did that a separate guy unconnected to that group of girls and presumably thinking I was a boy with my arm around another boy walked by the table and spat the word 'Fags' in our direction. So, in the space of two minutes I'd been called a dyke AND a fag. I felt so lucky that night in the pub that I'd never internalised any offhand homophobic comments that my parents made growing up, because they were so careful not to. That night in the pub I remember thinking, 'Wow. I really wish Wendy and James had raised everyone.' (I quickly remembered that no, that would make dating impossible. Everyone would be my siblings.)

The chances are, if you look in any way 'different', if people perceive you as anything other than 'normal', if you express same-sex affection unashamedly, then at some point you will hear these words directed at you. And it sucks. Even though my parents were unbelievably liberal, I'd be being naive if I said I hadn't got some battle wounds on my own internal landscape from living in a culture oriented towards heteronormativity (where heterosexuality and binary gender identities are implicitly considered the 'norm') while not being 'heteronormal' myself. Another thing that will happen in your life is that you will see, on the news and on social media, conversations played out regarding LGBTQ+ rights. You'll see entire countries voting on the legality and legitimacy of your love and your feelings. You'll see respectable-seeming people being given a public platform to calmly or not so calmly debate against your advocates/allies on the subject of your very humanity, your right to be viewed as an equal and valuable citizen. I wish I could personally come to your house and cover your eyes and put cotton in your ears when this nonsense comes on your screen. These opinions are toxic. They are the currency and symptoms of a scared, confused and aggressive faction of people who are wilfully ignorant to the multifacetedness of human nature, including their own. I am sorry more strength may be required of you than other people, in order for you to withstand the creeping tendrils of self-doubt or shame that hearing these bigots can cause, but I know that you have that strength.

Things are going to be great.

ADVICE TO MY YOUNGER SELF

I asked some of my funny friends who are comfortable with their sexualities to write messages to their younger selves. What would have been helpful for them to hear? Here is what they said.

TOM ALLEN

Hey you! You in the bow tie and the waistcoat carrying a briefcase! Stop putting yourself under so much pressure all the time. Take some time to f things up and don't you dare beat yourself up for doing it. Try and be kinder to yourself. But it's not enough that I'm telling you to do this. I know this won't solve it. Just remember no one will really care about your exam results. And speak to a therapist so they can reassure you that you're okay. And you're more than your school work. You're better than okay. And any feelings of negativity you have for yourself they're not okay. And they're definitely not your fault.

DANIELLA ISAACS

Recognise that your sexuality is yours and only yours. That recognition is incredibly freeing and sexy and exciting. Become aware of the heteronormative narrative you were force fed from birth as soon as possible. Question it. Break it down. Feel empowered and curious to learn more and more about who you are politically, socially and sexually (without anyone else dictating that for you). I would tell myself, if others judge you it is their ignorant way of shielding their own insecurities. I would tell myself, you deserve to feel free enough to be open and honest and curious and ever-changing right up until you're a gorgeous geriatric. Oh, and then I would remind myself: if you're privileged enough (like I luckily am) to be open about your sexuality, make it your duty to celebrate it and use it to help amplify others who remain silenced. That's how change begins.

SUZI RUFFELL

Hello Suzi, its Suzi from the future. Creepy!

Firstly you're dyslexic not stupid. You'll find this out at college.

So, I hate to be the one to break this to you but you haven't got a hoverboard and it doesn't look like they are happening any time soon. Sorry!

I know you are feeling a bit scared at the moment, it's hard having a secret, feeling like you can never relax or let your guard down in case people find out. It's exhausting and I know its making you a bit miserable. You will confront it though, you'll eventually tell everyone and it will be okay. A few people take a moment to get their heads around the idea but after a short while everything is fine. You get the things you dream of, the parts of life you are scared of missing out on because you feel different, you will fall in love and have lots of friends and find a job you love. The shame you feel about your sexuality does leave you, you become proud of who you are, in fact, you shout it from the rooftops. Try not to worry so much, read more, musicals are brilliant, ignore anyone that says they aren't, a fringe doesn't suit you no matter how many times you try and you do eventually get to see Alanis Morrisette live, it's in about 18 years and its still amazing.

Be kind to yourself, learn as much as possible and keep trying to make people laugh, that ends up being quite useful.

Love from me (you).
Ps— I know your biggest fear is telling Nan, she doesn't care that you're gay, it doesn't change your relationship and she loves you just as much!

SABRINA JALES

Being different is actually the best. That looking back it was all the stuff that I was initially embarrassed or shy about (being Pakistani, being gay ...) that ended up being my favourite parts of me. I'd tell me that, let's be honest, everyone is a little gay or a little straight or mostly straight or mostly gay but that life is barely ever binary and that goes for gender too. I'd tell me not to go to Le Chateau the summer before high school to femme up my new identity because let's be real that butterfly headband and skirt combo was never gonna work. And I'd also say in 2010 there will be a thing called Bitcoin invented. Buy a hundred thousand shares for 8 cents a share and sell them in 2018 when they hit $27,000 each. And I'd say don't be a monster. Donate half the money.

AND WHAT
WOULD I
SAY TO MY
YOUNGER
SELF?

I'D SAY ...

DEAR MAE,

You're about to head into puberty. It is going to feel like the world has been turned upside down. Suddenly all your incredible party tricks – like knowing all the lyrics to the theme from Fresh Prince, or being able to make the sound of an angry duck using only your hands – will lose their value among your friends at your all-girls' school. Your friends will suddenly value other things, namely, the attention of boys, having the right lip gloss, looking like the girls on the covers of magazines. Hormones will be raging, and everything will feel insane. You might feel as though, because you have short hair and aren't interested in those things, you have no value. You might feel unattractive or weird. Let me tell you – save yourself the pain of trying to conform. I know I can't stop you – you will grow your hair long for three ill-advised years, you will wear weird choker necklaces and at one stage you will even attempt to have your hair tied in multiple baubles on your head like Scary Spice. You will wear a perfume called Flirty and experiment with various levels of eyeliner. These will be unsuccessful looks.

Later in life, once everyone has calmed down after puberty, you'll find your place again and you can still have the attention of boys, even if you are exactly your androgynous self.

Quick tip: DON'T try to shoplift hair dye from the Bloor and Bathurst Shoppers Drug Mart in Toronto. You will get caught and it will be so stressful. DON'T get a tattoo of the word OATMEAL on your right wrist. It will upset your parents much more than it will aesthetically please you.

DO stay open and romantic, have as many relationships as your heart can handle, give them your all. You'll learn so much from every single person. Intimacy is the greatest thing on earth.

Try not to worry about how you look so much. Just focus on being kind to people and, crucially, to yourself. And try to recognise as soon as you can, that just because you don't look or feel like what we are told girls are supposed to be, and just because you don't look or feel like what we are told boys are supposed to be, it doesn't mean that you are a failed version of both. Maybe you're just something else, and that's okay.

When you are older you will write a book and you should be aware that it will take a lot longer than you previously anticipated to write it so maybe give yourself a bigger window of time to write it in.

LOVE,

MAE

P.S. You are allergic to coconut. That's why every time you eat it you get hives and diarrhoea. Figure this out sooner than age 29.

NOTES

CHAPTER 1: 21ˢᵀ CENTURY SEXUALITY

1. Dahlgreen, Will 2015, '1 in 2 young people say they are not 100% heterosexual'. YouGov, 16 August. https://yougov.co.uk/topics/lifestyle/articles-reports/2015/08/16/half-young-not-heterosexual, accessed 11 February 2019

CHAPTER 2: MAE'S SCHOOL OF SEXUALITY

2. Adams, H.E., Wright, L.W., & Lohr, B.A. 1996, 'Is homophobia associated with homosexual arousal?'. *Journal of Abnormal Psychology*, 105 (3), 440–5.
http://dx.doi.org/10.1037/0021-843X.105.3.440, accessed 11 February 2019

3. News Medical Life Sciences Staff 2006, '1,500 animals species practise homosexuality'. *News-Medical*, 23 October. https://www.news-medical.net/news/2006/10/23/1500-animal-species-practice-homosexuality.aspx, accessed 11 February 2019

CHAPTER 3: NATURE, NURTURE OR NEITHER?

4. Paredes-Ramos, P., Miquel, M., Coria-Avila, G.A. 2011, 'Juvenile play conditions sexual partner preference in adult female rats'.

Physiology & Behaviour, 104 (5), 1016-23 https://www.ncbi.nlm.nih.gov/pubmed/21777597, accessed 11 February 2019

5. Kendrick, K.M., Haupt, M.A., Hinton, M.R., Broad, K.D., Skinner J. D. 2001, 'Sex differences in the influence of mothers on the sociosexual preferences of their offspring.' *Hormones and Behavior*, 40 (2), 322–38. https://www.ncbi.nlm.nih.gov/pubmed/?term=km+kendrick+sex+differences+sociosexual, accessed 11 February 2019

6. D'Emilio, John 2009, interview with Sherry Wolf for *International Socialist Review*, January. https://isreview.org/issue/65/lgbt-liberation-build-broad-movement, accessed 11 February 2019

7. Stern, M., & Karraker, K. H. 1989, 'Sex stereotyping of infants: A review of gender labeling studies.' *Sex Roles: A Journal of Research*, 20(9-10), 501-522.
http://dx.doi.org/10.1007/BF00288198, accessed 11 February 2019

CHAPTER 4: IS EVERYTHING ON A SPECTRUM?

8. Kinsey, Alfred C., 'The Kinsey Scale'. Kinsey Institute. https://www.kinseyinstitute.org/research/publications/kinsey-scale.php, accessed 11 February 2019

9. Brotto, Loria 2015, 'Sexual orientation is much more complex than straight, gay or bisexual'. *Globe and Mail*, 21 June. https://www.theglobeandmail.com/life/health-and-fitness/health-advisor/sexual-orientation-is-much-more-complex-than-straight-gay-or-bisexual/article26053887/, accessed 11 February 2019

10. Chivers, Meredith 2005, 'A brief review and discussion of sex differences in the specificity of sexual arousal.' *Sexual and Relationship Therapy*, 20 October. https://www.researchgate.net/publication/228379474_A_brief_review_and_discussion_of_sex_differences_in_the_specificity_of_sexual_arousal, accessed 11 February 2019

11. Kinsey, Alfred 1948, *Sexual Behavior in the Human Male* (Philadelphia: W.B. Saunders Company), 651.

12. Hutcherson, Josh 2013, 'Straight Talker'. Interview with Shana Naomi Krochmal for *Out*, 9 October. https://www.out.com/movies/2013/10/09/josh-hutcherson-says-best-thing-his-hunger-games-character-might-be-threesome, accessed 11 February 2019

13. Cyrus, Miley 2015, 'Free to be Miley'. Interview with Amanda Petrusich for *Paper*, 9 June. http://www.papermag.com/free-to-be-miley-1427581961.html, accessed 11 February 2019

14. Rose, Ruby 2015, 'OITNB's Ruby Rose Schools Us on Gender Fluidity'. Interview with Jessie Mooney for *Elle*, 15 June. https://www.elle.com/culture/movies-tv/a28865/ruby-rose-oitnb/, accessed 11 February 2019

15. Ke$ha 2013, 'The Wild Child Finally Shows Her Softer Side'. *Seventeen*, February

16. Jackson, Elly 2014, 'La Roux: I don't get fame. I don't understand what you're supposed to do'. Interview with Tim Jonze for *Guardian*, 25 May. https://www.theguardian.com/music/2014/may/25/-sp-elly-jackson-i-dont-understand-fame, accessed 11 February 2019.

17. Lovato, Demi 2015, 'Pop Life'. Interview with Christine Werthman for *Complex*, Oct/Nov. https://www.complex.com/music/demi-lovato-interview-2015-cover-story, accessed 11 February 2019

CHAPTER 5: NEVER READ THE LABEL

18. Ochs, Robyn 2016, 'The definition of bisexuality (according to bi organisations, activists, and the community)'. Robyn Ochs, 18 April. https://robynochs.com/2016/04/18/the-definition-of-bisexuality-according-to-bi-2/, accessed 11 February 2019

CHAPTER 6: COMING OUT (AND GOING BACK IN)

19. Stenberg, Amandla 2018, interview with King Princess for *Wonderland*, 18 June. https://www.wonderlandmagazine.com/2018/06/18/amandla-stenberg-wonderland/, accessed 11 February 2019

GLOSSARY

Here is a glossary that includes some of the terms used in the book that you may want clarification on. These are not detailed definitions, and it's by no means an exhaustive list of all the many terms and identities out there, so please google if you want more information!

Agender – a person who sees themselves as existing outside the traditional concepts of a male and female gender, or sees themselves as being genderless.

Androgynous – this is when someone has elements of both masculinity and femininity in their gender identity.

Asexual – a person who has little or no interest in sexual behaviour. Not all asexual people are 'aromantic' – many of them still have romantic relationships and asexuality can vary in degrees

Binary – binary means 'of two things'. The gender binary refers to the (in my opinion outdated!) distinction of sex and gender into two opposite forms of masculine and feminine. The idea that you can only be one of two things.

Bisexual – historically, this has meant a person who is attracted to both men and women. As we move away from the gender binary, however, 'bisexual' is now sometimes used to describe someone who is attracted to many or all genders. People often prefer to use 'bisexual' when they mean 'pansexual' (attracted to all genders) because people are more familiar

with the term bisexual. To be 'bisexual' you don't have to be attracted to different genders with an equal intensity. For instance, you may be sexually attracted to both men and women, but only romantically attracted to men.

Cisgender – a person whose gender identity matches their biological sex assigned at birth. So in other words, not transgender.

Coming out – this is what we call it when someone shares their sexuality or gender identity with others (friends, colleagues, etc.).

Cultural norms – the standards we live by. They are the shared expectations and rules that guide behaviour of people within social groups. Cultural norms are learned and reinforced from parents, friends, teachers and others while growing up in a society.

Demisexual – someone who is demisexual experiences little or no sexual attraction to others until a strong emotional connection is formed.

Drag queen – someone who performs femininity often theatrically. There is a vibrant drag queen culture – get out there and see some drag shows!

Femme – this is often used to describe a feminine-presenting queer

person. It refers to someone who identifies themselves as feminine physically, mentally or emotionally.

Gay – people who are primarily attracted to members of the same sex and/or gender.

Gender identity – the internal perception we have of our own gender, and how we label that. Some gender identities include: man, woman, nonbinary, genderqueer, trans, and more. People often confuse 'gender' with biological sex, which refers to the anatomy we're born with but can be different to our 'gender identity'.

Gender/sexuality spectrum – this refers to the broad range of identities and feelings we can have.

Gender pronouns – for example 'he', 'she', 'them', 'ze' – these are the words that people use to describe us if they're not using our name. 'They' and 'ze' are gender neutral and can be used to refer to someone who is transgender or doesn't feel comfortable being addressed with feminine or masculine pronouns.

Sexually fluid/fluid sexuality – this is the idea that your sexuality and sexual preference can change in your lifetime, and in many cases is dependent on situations. If you say you're 'sexually fluid', you're recognising the potential of your sexuality to change, and that it's not necessarily a fixed thing.

Heteronormative – this refers to the idea that it is often assumed, by individuals or in society, that everyone is heterosexual (for example, instinctively asking a man if he has a girlfriend). For the most part, we live in a heteronormative society still, in which most things are geared towards that assumption, and the assumption of a gender binary (men are masculine, women are feminine). The fact that LGBTQ+ people have to "come out" is partly because of this assumption that everyone is straight.

Homophobe – someone who has a negative attitude towards LGBTQ+ people or non-heterosexual sexual/romantic activity. This could be fear, anger, hatred, discomfort, etc.

Homophobia – an umbrella term for the range of negative feelings a homophobe feels.

Intersex – a term for someone possessing a combination of chromosomes, hormones, internal sex organs or genitals, which are different from the expected patterns of male and female.

Lesbian – a woman who is attracted to other women.

LGBTQ+ – this refers to the longer initialism of LGBTQQIAAP (lesbian, gay, bisexual, transgender, queer, questioning, intersex, allies, asexual, pansexual). The PLUS (+) ensures that we will always be inclusive of all identities to make our community feel welcomed and make sure that nobody is left out.

Orientation – sexual orientation is different to your gender or gender identity, it means who you're attracted to and want to have sexual or romantic relationships with. Some sexual orientations include gay, lesbian, straight, bisexual and asexual.

Pansexual – a person who is attracted (romantically, sexually or both) to members of all gender identities. 'Pansexual' can be shortened to 'pan'.

Queer – 'queer' used to be a derogatory term, so some people still aren't keen on it, but it has also now been embraced by much of the LGBTQ+ community as a term to simply mean 'not straight'. I personally like it a lot.

Sexuality – a person's sexual feelings.

Skoliosexual – people who are primarily attracted to genderqueer/ transgender/nonbinary people.

Stereotype – this refers to the (largely damaging) tendency we have to hold an oversimplified image or idea of a group of people. For example, 'women talk a lot', 'men are good at sports'.

Straight – another word for heterosexual, a person who is primarily attracted to people who are not their same sex/gender.

Trans* – an umbrella term that incorporates many identities outside socially defined gender norms.

Transgender – a person who lives as a member of a gender that is different to the one they were assigned at birth based on their anatomical sex.

RESOURCES

Stonewall
www.stonewall.org.uk
Charity campaigning for lesbian, gay, bi and
trans equality

Switchboard
www.switchboard.lgbt
Helpline for LGBTQ+ people

The Mix
www.themix.org.uk
Essential support and advice for young people on
everything from gender and sexuality to mental health
and lifestyle

Childline
https://www.childline.org.uk/info-advice/your-feelings/
sexual-identity/sexual-orientation/
Advice on sexuality, coming out, bullying
and discrimination

It Gets Better Project

https://itgetsbetter.org/

A nonprofit organisation aiming to uplift, empower and connect lesbian, gay, bisexual, transgender and queer youth around the globe

MindOut

https://www.mindout.org.uk/

Mental health service run by and for the LGBTQ+ community

ACKNOWLEDGEMENTS

Special thanks to: Laura Horsley, Debbie Foy and everyone at Hachette, Tiffany Agbeko, Camilla Cole, Lindsay Barton, Monica Heisey, Rose Johnson, Adam Hess, Gaby Leith, Nicole Simon, Dr Meg-John Barker, Sabrina Jalees, Daniella Isaacs, Tom Allen, Suzi Ruffell, Bertie Peek, Joe Hampson. And again my parents Wendy and James, and my brother Joseph.